D0109727

SUPERMAN

★ VERSUS ★

THE KU KLUX KLAN

THE TRUE STORY OF HOW THE ICONIC SUPERHERO BATTLED THE MEN OF HATE

BY RICK BOWERS

SCHOLASTIC INC.
New York Toronto London Auckland
Sydney Mexico City New Delhi Hong Kong

With profound love: Wynn, Neva, Helen and Joy.

ISBN 978-0-545-43745-5

12 11 10 9 8 7 6 5 4 3 2
12 13 14 15 16 17/0

Printed in the U.S.A.   23

First Scholastic printing, February 2012

Nancy Laties Feresten, *Editor*
James Hiscott, Jr., *Art Director/Designer*
Lori Epstein, *Senior Illustrations Editor*

Book design by James Hiscott, Jr.
Text is set in Garamond Premier Pro; display text in Knockout.

ILLUSTRATION CREDITS

10, Special Collections, Michael Schwartz Library at Cleveland State University; 18, American Stock/Getty Images; 24, Private collection; 32, Berenice Abbott/Miriam and Ira D. Wallach Division of Art, Prints and Photographs/The New York Public Library; 38, Private collection; 48, Arthur Rothstein/FSA/State Archives of Florida/Library of Congress; 56, Library of Congress; 62, EPIC/The Kobal Collection; 68, Underwood & Underwood/Corbis; 78, Private collection; 86, Carl Iwasaki/Time Life Pictures/Getty Images; 92, Private collection; 98, Private collection; 106, Keystone Features/Getty Images; 114, The University of Maryland Broadcasting Archives; 124, Ed Clark/Time & Life Pictures/Getty Images; 132, Leonard Detrick/NY Daily News Archive via Getty Images; 140, Private collection; 150, Private collection.

All insert images courtesy of private collection unless otherwise noted below: insert 4, Lippert Pictures/Getty Images; insert 5, DC Comics/Warner Bros/The Kobal Collection

CONTENTS

FROM THE AUTHOR

RESEARCHING AND WRITING *Superman versus the Ku Klux Klan* was like traveling back in time. To make the journey into the world of old superheroes, I pored through the vast archives of great libraries, universities, and the extensive personal compilations of dedicated comic book collectors and dealers. To track the birth and rebirths of the Ku Klux Klan, I studied the original writings of the first KKK supporters, the works of prominent historians, and the faded spy reports of anti-Klan infiltrators. I felt a great sense of excitement when these two powerful stories finally intersected at the Clan of the Fiery Cross—the 16-part *Adventures of Superman* radio show that pitted the Man of Steel against the men of hate. At that point the flow of history ran as strong and wild as the currents of two intersecting rivers. I'll never forget the thrill of uncovering rare documents describing the extensive preparation the radio producers conducted to prepare for the controversial broadcasts. I'll never forget the chills that ran through me while reading FBI-infiltrator reports of KKK meetings— reports capturing plans to attack and murder inno-cent people simply because of their skin color. Through all the historical files, infiltration documents, and interviews, I always sought to sort out myth from fact and capture the essence of truth. In the end I hope you enjoy reading the story as much as I enjoyed writing it. I hope you find *Superman versus the Ku Klux Klan* both informative and interesting and that you, too, will one day embark on your own journey back in time.

This book would not have been possible without the support of many talented and dedicated friends and colleagues. The first thank you goes to my editor at National Geographic, Nancy Feresten, who suggested the original idea and guided the process from start to finish. Special thanks also to her talented editorial ace Kate Olesin, whose organizational skills kept the process moving forward even when it wanted to pause. Also special thanks to the librarians and researchers at the Library of Congress, the University of Minnesota's Elmer L. Andersen Library, and the Schomburg Center for Research in Black Culture in New York. These diligent protectors of our shared history opened up archives and tracked down documents, helping me locate valuable papers that had been collecting dust for decades. Extra special thanks to professor Steven Weisenburger of Southern Methodist University in Dallas for sharing his files on the Ku Klux Klan infiltration in Atlanta as well as the infiltration of the neo-Nazi Columbians. His work dissecting the underlying ideology of home-grown fascism continues to provide essential awareness of the continuing threat. Also, enormous gratitude to the private collector who allowed us to photograph and share her glimpses of some of the most precious and important comic books in the world. And finally to all the family members and friends who listened to my stories, read the early versions, and shared their ideas, your support is cherished.

THE BIRTH OF SUPERMAN

In the early 1930s newspaper headlines told of the hardships of the Great Depression. Americans fortunate enough to have jobs fretted about losing them. Those who had lost their jobs often turned to breadlines and soup kitchens just to keep from starving. In Europe the desperate economic climate had given rise to fascist leaders who preached the superiority of a master race and advocated the elimination of all "inferior" races. In a tight-knit Jewish enclave in Cleveland, Ohio, a shy teenager was working on a solution. To his mind, the world needed a superhero.

Glenville was a pleasant community of nice homes and big backyards, as well as a safe haven for its Jewish residents.

CHAPTER 1

KOSHER DELIS & DISTANT GALAXIES

WALKING DOWN THE HALLWAY of Glenville High, Jerry Siegel braced for another day of disappointment. It was only 8:30 in the morning, and the 17-year-old science fiction aficionado was already counting the hours to the final bell. The pretty girl with the long, brown hair and flashing eyes would no doubt turn away from his glances. The student editor of the award-winning school newspaper, the *Torch*, would probably reject his latest story idea. The swaggering guys on the football team and the cliquish cheerleaders on their arms would not even acknowledge his existence. At least after school Jerry could hustle to his house at 10622 Kimberly Avenue, bound up to his hideaway in the attic, pick up a science fiction magazine, and lose himself in a fantasy world of mad scientists and rampaging monsters, space explorers and alien invaders, time travelers and spectral beings.

Jerry loved science fiction. Ever since he was a kid he had buried himself in a new breed of magazines with titles like *Weird Tales* and *Amazing Stories*. Full of dense print and crude illustrations, these simple, low-budget publications were magic to him. The smudged type on that thin paper told stories of intergalactic warfare, futuristic civilizations, and brilliant new technologies that promised a brighter and better world.

These astounding tales were attracting a growing audience of teenage fans across the country. They referred to their magazines as zines and shared their reactions and ideas through the mail. For Jerry, zines were the ultimate escape from his humdrum existence at school and the tension at home with his mother, who constantly babied him and worried that he was too much of a dreamer to make it in a harsh world.

Jerry had to admit that his future did not look all that bright. Because he lacked the grades and the money to go to college, the world ahead often seemed as bleak as the coldest, darkest reaches of outer space.

Jerry Siegel was the youngest of six children born to Mitchell and Sarah Siegel. Like so many other Jewish immigrants, Mitchell and Sarah had fled persecution in Europe to build a new life in America. After arriving from Lithuania, the couple had changed their name from Segalovich to fit in more easily in their adopted homeland. At first Mitchell worked as a sign painter and dreamed of becoming an artist. But with a growing family to support, jobs scarce, and money tight, he gave up his dream of painting beautiful works of art. Instead he opened a haberdashery, or secondhand-clothing store, near the factories in the old Jewish ghetto of Cleveland. Mitchell worked long hours, saved his money, and eventually moved the family out of the ghetto and into a comfortable, three-story, wood-frame house in Glenville, a close-knit neighborhood of nice homes, spacious front porches, and big backyards. Set amid rambling green hills and gurgling streams that meandered to Lake Erie, Glenville was the American dream come true for its tens of thousands of Jewish residents.

Glenville was also a protective cocoon for those residents—a safe haven from the prejudice that lurked just outside its borders. Sure, there were plenty of good, hardworking Christian people out there, but some Christians called Jews insulting names like kike and hebe and instructed their children to stay away from those kinds of kids. The classifieds in the *Cleveland Plain Dealer* were filled with job ads bluntly stating "No Jews Need Apply." Country clubs in exclusive neighborhoods refused to accept Jewish members. There were even hate groups that called for the kinds of mass-removal programs that the Siegels thought they had escaped when they left Europe. In fact, Jews could simply turn on their radios to hear the Radio Priest, Father Charles Coughlin, spew anti-Semitic tirades from the National Shrine of the Little Flower Parish in Royal Oak, Michigan, just 180 miles from Glenville. A frequent speaker at mass rallies in Cleveland, Coughlin organized his most loyal followers into Christian Front organizations to oppose equality for Jewish Americans.

As the Great Depression wreaked economic havoc on the nation, another frightening fringe organization was becoming more and more active. With unemployment at a record high and clashes between striking workers and employers turning into bloody melees, the Ku Klux Klan (KKK) sought to exploit public fear. Preaching a gospel of racism and religious intolerance, the KKK called upon white protestant men to band together to fight the Jew's demand for social acceptance, the Negro's plea for just treatment, and the immigrant's call for decent jobs and fair pay. To keep up with the times, this secret society of hooded vigilantes had expanded its traditional hate list from Negroes, Jews, and Catholics to include union organizers, liberal politicians, civil rights advocates, crusading journalists, and supporters of the New Deal—President Franklin

Roosevelt's program to restore the economy by putting people to work. As tensions rose, new recruits came forward to join the nation's most militant defender of white protestant rule. Although the KKK recruited only members who were white and protestant, it boasted of standing for the principle of "100 percent Americanism."

On summer days the streets of Glenville buzzed with kids riding bikes, skipping rope, and playing stickball or hide-and-seek. On summer evenings teenage boys and girls walked hand in hand down the sidewalks, and gaggles of kids hung out on spacious front porches, told jokes, flirted, and talked about the future. Throughout the week pedestrians flowed down lively East 105th Street, where Solomon's Delicatessen piled corned beef and pastrami high on fresh rye bread and Old World restaurants served classic European fare like brisket, cheese blintzes, matzo ball soup, and lox and bagels. On Saturdays, worshippers flocked to more than 25 synagogues, the men wearing the traditional yarmulke to cover their heads and the women dressed in the fashions of the day. The jewel of Glenville was the grand Jewish Center of Anshe Emeth (a synagogue) at East 105th and Grantwood Avenue, a modern building with a sculpture of the Star of David crowning its roof. It was the central gathering place for the community—the place to go to shoot basketball, to swim laps, or to take classes on subjects ranging from Hebrew tradition to American culture. By the early 1930s more than half of Cleveland's Jewish population lived in Glenville, and more than 80 percent of the 1,600 kids at Glenville High were Jewish.

JERRY SIEGEL WAS DIFFERENT from most of the other kids in Glenville. While they were playing ball in the street, shooting hoops at the community center, or shopping on 105th Street, Jerry was holed up in the attic with his precious zines. He also loved to take in the movies at the Crown Theater, just a couple blocks from his house, or at the red-carpeted and balconied Uptown Theatre farther up 105th. Scrunched in his seat with a sack of popcorn in his lap and his eyes fixed on the screen, he marveled as the dashing actor Douglas Fairbanks donned a black cape and mask to become the leaping, lunging, sword-wielding Zorro. Jerry admired Fairbanks and all the other leading men—those strong, fearless, valiant he-man characters who took care of the bad guys and took care of the gorgeous women too. Jerry worshipped Clark Gable and Kent Taylor, whose names he would later combine to form Clark Kent.

Jerry usually sat in darkened theaters alone as he absorbed stories, tracked dialogue, and marveled at the characters. After the movies he would walk to the newsstands on St. Claire Avenue to pick up a pulp-fiction novel or a zine. Soaking in every line of narrative and dialogue, he would read the books and magazines cover to cover—then read them again. Turning to his secondhand typewriter, he would dash off letters to the editors, critiquing the stories and suggesting themes for future editions. He would scour the classified sections for the names and addresses of other science fiction fans and send them letters in which he shared his ideas for stories, plots, and characters. For kids like Jerry, science fiction provided a community—a network of fans bound together by a common passion.

One of Jerry's favorite books was Philip Wylie's *Gladiator*. Initially published in 1930, it was the first science fiction novel to introduce a character with superhuman powers. Jerry moved through the swollen river of words like an Olympian swimmer, devouring the description of the protagonist, Hugo Danner, whose bones and skin were so dense that he was more like steel than flesh, with the strength to hurl giant boulders, the speed to outrun trains, and the leaping ability of a grasshopper. Danner's life is a tortured pursuit of the question of whether to use his powers for good or evil. That made Jerry think about how hard it was to choose right over wrong.

Then there was that unforgettable image of the flying man—the one he had seen on the cover of *Amazing Stories*. Jerry would hang on to that image for the rest of his life. The flying man, clad in a tight red outfit and wearing a leather pilot's helmet, soared through the sunny sky and smiled down on a futuristic village filled with technological marvels. From the ground, a pretty, smiling girl waved a handkerchief at the airborne man and marveled at his fantastic abilities. In this edition of *Amazing Stories* Jerry saw a thrilling new world of scientific advances and social harmony— a perfect green and sunny utopia to be ushered in by creative geniuses with more brains than brawn, more natural imagination than school-injected facts, more good ideas than good looks. Jerry wanted to help create that utopia. Luckily, he had a partner in his quest.

During the era of silent films, actor Douglas Fairbanks played the swashbuckling Zorro.

CHAPTER 2

KINDRED SPIRITS & CREATIVE FORCES

JOE SHUSTER WAS A fellow science fiction fanatic, a talented illustrator, and another skinny, bashful kid with thick glasses and no girlfriends. Jerry and Joe were kindred spirits and tireless collaborators. Sequestered in an attic work space after school and on weekends, the boys spent hours talking about science fiction, conjuring up story ideas, and drawing illustrations. Over time they would create a world of mad scientists and futuristic space travelers, smooth-talking detectives and supernatural beings. Although he could draw a bit, Jerry generally took the role of writer, his more assertive personality driving the action. Writing in pithy sentences that could be squeezed into small narrative boxes and thought bubbles, he would conjure the concept, plot the story line, and develop the narrative. As the illustrator, Joe would envision the characters and scenes and then put pencil to paper as he brought the characters to life on cheap, brown butcher paper laid across his mother's favorite cutting board.

Early in 1932 Jerry and Joe went to work on their own typewritten magazine titled *Science Fiction: The Advanced Guard of Future Civilization.* Once they had their densely typed, roughly illustrated master copy in hand, they dashed off to the library to mimeograph copies and began mailing them to fellow fans within the free-ranging science fiction network. *Science Fiction* would also be sent to the publishers of the best zines, in hopes that one of them would purchase a piece of content, or, at least, recognize the talent of the young creators.

The third edition of *Science Fiction* featured a story entitled "The Reign of the Super-Man," in which a bald, diabolical chemist sets out to use a substance derived from a meteor to turn himself into an evil genius with the power to dominate the world. Although most of the stories in *Science Fiction* were written by Jerry and illustrated by Joe, "The Reign of the Super-Man" was signed with the byline Herbert Fine. The two amateurs probably thought the pen name was a professional touch that would create the illusion that there was another writer in their limited stable of contributors. Plus, it added a bit of protection against any prejudiced publishers who might like the story but suspect that the writers were Jewish based on their real names.

Jerry and Joe's "The Reign of the Super-Man" played off the grim realities of the Great Depression. In the story, treacherous Professor Smalley lures destitute, homeless men from soup kitchens to serve as guinea pigs for his hideous experiments: "With a contemptuous sneer on his face, Professor Smalley watched the wretched unfortunates file past him. To him, who had come of rich parents and had never been forced to face the rigors of life, the miserableness of these men seemed deserved."

It was a good tale, but it was not the page-turner the duo had hoped for. What was it? Jerry and Joe would tackle that question later. The pair were in what should have been their last year at Glenville High, and the world of work was looming ahead—although they would both end up repeating that year because they lacked the grades to graduate.

In addition to hanging out with Joe, Jerry loved to spend time with his dad, Mitchell, who supported his youngest son's creative endeavors. Maybe this support stemmed from Mitchell's own abandoned dream of being a painter. Or perhaps he was just going easier on his youngest child than he had on the others, who had been expected to work part-time at the haberdashery, to do well in school, and to prepare to find good jobs (the boys) or good husbands (the girls). Then, in an instant, the family's life changed forever.

On June 2, 1932, just after closing time, a neighboring merchant noticed that the haberdashery's door was ajar. The interior lights were on, but Mitchell Siegel was nowhere in sight. The concerned shopkeeper pushed open the door and found Mitchell sprawled on the floor behind the counter—dead. The money in the cash register was gone, as were the three thugs who had robbed him. Initial police reports suggested that Siegel had been shot in the chest and found in a pool of blood behind the cash register. The coroner's report later amended the scenario: Mitchell had suffered a fatal heart attack during the robbery. Either way, the Siegel family would never be the same.

Jerry's mother fell into a deep depression. Her message to the children was cold and absolute: Never mention the robbery to anyone. All that the neighbors needed to know was that their father had died of a heart attack. Period. Relatives flocked to Sarah's side, tried to console the kids, made sure that the bills were paid, and shook their heads over the tragedy. With the Great Depression bearing down, Mitchell's income gone, and money tighter than ever, the family did the best they could. Devastated by the loss of his dad, Jerry withdrew even more into his science fiction world.

But a fire burned within him. He was more determined than ever to make it in the publishing business. He would work tirelessly to honor the memory of his hardworking father. He had no way of knowing that success was not far beyond the horizon. The shy, grieving, self-conscious, seemingly powerless teen could not foresee that his imagination would conjure up a muscular, all-powerful, super human who could deflect bullets, bend steel in his bare hands, soar into the sky, and protect the little guy from thugs and hoodlums like those who had caused his father's death.

An early version of the Superman story featured a crime-fighting character who lacked truly amazing powers.

CHAPTER 3

THE MAGIC OF THE MIX

BY 1934 NEWLY MINTED high school graduates Jerry Siegel and Joe Shuster were operating their own comic art business. While their fellow Glenville graduates were taking introductory philosophy classes on college campuses, operating drill presses in factories, or searching for any work they could find, these offbeat science fiction devotees were pitching their ideas to professional editors and publishers. Fancying himself the business brains of the two-man outfit, Jerry took the lead in managing the enterprise. Concepts for new characters had to be put down on paper and sent out. Push. Letters had to be written to editors and publishers looking for content. Push. Push. Their primary targets were the syndicates that distributed comic strips to newspapers and the companies that were introducing a new kind of publication: comic books.

Jerry and Joe's story of the Super-Man—that diabolical scientist who conducted gruesome experiments on unsuspecting homeless men—was still incubating in their minds. Then, according to Superman lore, late one night in the summer of 1934, the answer hit Jerry like a lightning bolt.

They had it backward. The world had no need for an evil superman. The world needed a good superman—a trustworthy and powerful ally who would come to the rescue of regular people by protecting them from ruthless criminals, cheating businessmen, and corrupt politicians. With millions of people out of work, the streets full of crime, the stock market in ruins, and a war brewing in Europe, readers were starved for hope, inspiration, and a sense of power. A good superman could provide all that.

ACCORDING TO THE LORE, the essence of the character—the one the world would come to know—flashed into Jerry's mind that restless night with the force of one of those sci-fi meteors crashing to Earth. In point of fact, the epiphany of the good superman sparked a long collaboration that would lead to the iteration of the character known today. The day after the epiphany, Jerry ran to Joe's house, and the two began evolving the basic story line of the good superman. The next full-fledged version came several months later with the creation of an all-too-human hero the collaborators modestly dubbed "The Most Astounding Fiction Character of All Time!" This superman was strong, agile, and heroic but lacked extraordinary super-powers that would differentiate him from other heroes.

The few publishers who considered the proposal rejected it. Frustrated with the failure, Joe went into a rage and began destroying the manuscript. Jerry intervened but managed to save only the cover. The cover, showing the Superman leaping at a gun-wielding thug, was eerily reminiscent of Mitchell Siegel's death. Still not quite right. The work continued.

As the writer, Jerry took the lead in developing the now-classic story line that finally emerged. Superman is born on the planet Krypton. His scientist father places him in a small rocket ship and launches him toward

Earth just moments before Krypton erupts in devastating earthquakes and explosions that kill all the inhabitants. The spacecraft lands on Earth, where people discover the baby and take him to an orphanage in a small midwestern town. A family named Kent adopts him, gives him the name Clark, and raises him on a farm. After realizing the possibilities of his superhuman powers, Clark moves to the big city of Metropolis and becomes a reporter for a great metropolitan newspaper.

In times of trouble Clark sheds his street clothes and peels off his glasses to become Superman. He uses his powers to leap great heights, to hoist huge weights, to deflect bullets, to soar into the sky, and to subdue criminals. His only motives are to protect the innocent, to bring the guilty to justice, and to crusade for a better world. After saving the day, Superman returns to his guise as the mild-mannered Clark, who works at the newspaper with a gutsy "girl reporter" named Lois Lane. But Lois has little time for bespectacled, nerdy Clark. She only has eyes for Superman.

Sensing that the character was special, the two creators worked feverishly to fill in the details of his persona. Before long the full picture was on the page. Superman had his rugged good looks, his shock of blue-black hair, his muscular physique, his flowing red cape, and the bold S insignia on his chest. Joe designed his uniform as a cross between a spaceman suit and a classic circus performer outfit—down to the blue tights, red shorts, and cape. He skillfully captured each of Superman's actions in single comic panels: the caped crusader raising his arms toward the heavens, leaping off the ground with incredible strength, soaring upward at supersonic speed, and landing with both feet firmly planted on the ground. The Man of Steel—also called the Man of Tomorrow in those early days—stands tall, hands on his hips, bullets bouncing off his chest, as befuddled, gun-packing gangsters fire shot after harmless shot. In time the classic image would evolve: The handsome, smiling superhero would save Lois Lane from all kinds of danger, hoist her in his arms, soar over the flickering lights of Metropolis, and deliver her safely home.

To breathe life into the Superman character, Jerry and Joe drew upon their love of science fiction, their passion for movies, their fascination for books, and their experiences growing up Jewish during the Great Depression. The Greek and Roman myths they learned at school featured heroes with superhuman strength. Strange visitors from distant planets were common in the science fiction stories they devoured night and day. Daredevil heroes clad in masks and capes were all the rage in the movies they watched at the Crown and the Uptown. Even heroes with dual identities were commonplace on the screen and in print. The silent screen character Zorro was the alter ego of Don Diego de la Vega, a sissified aristocrat who ate, drank, and dressed the dandy to throw off suspicion of his role as the night-riding avenger. The Shadow, a pulp magazine character, was the alter ego of Kent Allard, a famed pilot who fought for the French during World War I. Just as the name Clark Kent was a cross between actors Clark Gable and Kent Taylor, the name of the mythical city of Metropolis came from the 1927 silent film of the same name. For Superman, the magic was in the mix.

Jerry and Joe's Jewish heritage deeply influenced the makeup of Superman too. The all-American superhero reflected many of the beliefs and values of Jewish immigrants of the day. Like them, Superman had come to America from a foreign world. Like them, he longed to fit in to his strange new surroundings. Superman also seemed to embody the Jewish principle of *tzedakah*—a command to serve the less fortunate and to stand up for the weak and exploited—and the concept of *tikkun olam,* the mandate to do good works (literally, to "repair a broken world"). Even the language of Superman had Jewish origins. Before Superman is blasted off the dying planet of Krypton, Superman's father, Jor-El, names his son Kal-El. In ancient Hebrew the suffix *El* means "all that is God."

Then there is the Moses connection. Just before Krypton explodes, Superman's parents place him in a crib-size rocket and launch him toward Earth to be raised by loving strangers. In the Old Testament, after Pharaoh decrees that all newborn Jewish males be killed, Moses's mother places him in a crib-size basket and launches him down the Nile River to be raised by others. Just as Pharaoh's daughter rescues the infant Moses from the bulrushes and nurtures him as her own, the Kents find and raise Superman on Earth. The Superman story also resembles the tale of Rabbi Maharal of Prague, who created his own superman, called the Golem, to protect the people of the Jewish ghetto from hostile Christians.

While Superman was a complex conglomeration of influences, Jerry and Joe left plenty to readers' imaginations. What Superman *wasn't* was just as important as what he *was.* The character had no clear ethnic background, no hint of an accent or dialect, no stated religious preference, and no political affiliation. The Superman character offered a little bit to everyone. Coming from a distant planet, he was the ultimate foreigner. Raised in the midwestern heartland, he was the quintessential American. Growing up in a small town, he was rural at heart. Moving to a big city, he became more sophisticated and worldly. He was both weak and strong. His meek, mild alter ego, Clark Kent, was a sheepish bumbler, but he was always ready to transform himself into the all-powerful superhero. So Superman was relevant to the prairie farmer, the urban factory worker, the white-collar insurance salesman, the hardworking waitress, and the struggling immigrant. Millions of ordinary people struggling through the Depression could imagine themselves shedding their plain, run-of-the-mill exteriors to reveal their real power within. True, Superman had descended from the heavens with the power of a god. His intention was godly too—to protect humanity from its own worst instincts. But Superman had characteristics the masses could relate to. He could beam with a smile, burst into anger, and form lasting friendships. Beneath it all Superman seemed like a regular guy.

Superman was also a creation of his times. To keep up with those times, Jerry and Joe often spent Saturdays flipping through out-of-town newspapers and national newsmagazines for ideas at the Cleveland Public Library. The headlines described crisis after crisis. The New York Stock Exchange had lost 90 percent of its value. Millions of Americans were out of work. A midwestern drought had engulfed prairie farms in the Dust Bowl, and desperate farmers had to pack up their starving families and head to California to start anew. The international news was no more comforting. Headlines warned of economic collapse in global markets, the rise of fascist regimes in Europe, and the new communist experiment in the Soviet Union. The whole world seemed to be heading toward an explosion.

Despite the challenges, Jerry and Joe found hope in President Franklin D. Roosevelt, who had declared in his 1932 inaugural address that "the only thing we have to fear is fear itself." The two teenagers liked the sound of Roosevelt's promise of "a new deal for America." FDR proposed a series of government programs designed to create jobs, to restore the economy, and to address a range of social ills. In his popular fireside chats, broadcast on all the major radio networks in an era before the invention of television,

Roosevelt spoke in plain language that resonated with common men and women. As children of the Depression, Jerry and Joe saw hope in FDR's pledge to help the average person cope with the "hazards and vicissitudes of life," to provide some measure of protection "to the average citizen and to his family against the loss of a job and against poverty-ridden old age." Superman could get behind goals like that.

While FDR had broad public support, fierce critics charged him with either ignoring the national crisis or overreacting to it. Conservative opponents called him a socialist and formed the American Liberty League to derail his welfare programs. Radical opponents wrote off FDR's relief initiatives as "mere crumbs" and demanded sweeping "share the wealth" programs that involved confiscating the money and property of the rich and redistributing it to the poor. Answering the critics, Roosevelt declared:

A few timid people, who fear progress, will try to give you new and strange names for what we are doing. Sometimes they will call it "fascism," sometimes "communism," sometimes "regimentation," sometimes "socialism..." I believe that what we are doing today is a necessary fulfillment of what Americans have always been doing— a fulfillment of old and tested American ideals.

So Jerry and Joe plucked elements from the world around them to stir into their Superman stew. For the most part, however, Superman's millions of fans would ignore his origins. For them the Man of Steel would simply be the defender of the little man and woman—and a big problem for the forces of evil in the world.

In the 1920s New York City newsstands overflowed with magazines for a growing range of seemingly insatiable readers.

CHAPTER 4

BOOTLEG WHISKEY & PRINTER'S INK

SUPERMAN WAS FASTER than a speeding bullet. His rise to fame was not. The right people would have to come along, and the right circumstances would have to present themselves, before the world could meet Jerry and Joe's new character. Some 500 miles from Glenville was a place where the optimal conditions for the launch of this new kind of superhero had been brewing—the high-energy world of New York City publishing.

In the early 20th century the Big Apple had changed rapidly from a crass and overpopulated commercial center to the self-proclaimed "greatest city in the world," and the printed word, photo, and hand-drawn illustration were among its most important commodities. Amid the grit and glamour, clamor and chaos of the bustling sidewalks stood a loosely organized network of newsstands—thousands of gathering places where customers looked through rack after rack of magazines and pulp books covering an ever-expanding range of passions and pursuits. From the offices of the great skyscrapers, visionary publishers launched entire companies dedicated to serving specific slices of readers' expanding interests and hobbies. From the bowels of the city's grimy manufacturing hubs, printing presses rolled out a steady stream of books, magazines, and newspapers in currents as strong as those of the nearby Hudson River. For the professional types among the waves of immigrants entering the United States through the halls of Ellis Island, and for their children, the publishing industry represented a chance at getting a thinking man's job.

The advent of cheap and efficient color printing technology, coupled with car and truck delivery to newsstands and stores, pushed the growth of the publishing business. By the freewheeling 1920s printing presses rolled out vast quantities of titles such as *Indolent Kisses* and *Heart Throbs* to *True Detective* and *Time*. Ambitious publishers, persnickety editors, creative writers, talented illustrators, and hardworking pressmen served a market of seemingly insatiable readers.

While the disheartening effect of the Great Depression put a damper on the New York publishing trade, the great newspapers, newsmagazines, and popular magazines survived even as their weaker competitors vanished. And even as the quest for profits grew more brutal and the scramble for jobs intensified, New York remained the center of the publishing industry in America. It offered the enterprising entrepreneur an opportunity to run with an idea, to forge a market, and to make a living. The keys to success were twofold: a good idea and a fighting spirit.

In 1933 an out-of-work, would-be publisher and newspaper comic strip aficionado named Max Gaines (he had changed his name from Maxwell Ginzburg to sound less Jewish) came up with one of those good ideas: to take daily and weekly comic strips from newspapers; to arrange them on pages of cheap newsprint; to staple the pages between glossy, four-color cardboard covers; and to market the books to kids. The Eastern

Color Printing Company agreed to test Gaines's concept and produced 35,000 copies of *Famous Funnies, Series 1,* for distribution as a free promotion to department stores. The entire print run vanished almost overnight, and Eastern rushed *Famous Funnies, Series 2,* to newsstands. This time the company sold copies for a dime apiece.

Eastern then launched an entire series of comic compilation books without the services of the disappointed Gaines. But the enterprising businessman—showing that fighting spirit—struck a profit-sharing deal with the McClure Newspaper Syndicate and set out to launch a competing line. As Gaines's new titles became profitable, more publishers began bundling books of comic strip reprints and selling them at newsstands and dime stores. Before long the backlog of available newspaper strips had been exhausted, and existing content for new compilations was scarce.

That's when the trailblazing publisher of National Allied Publications began hiring new writers and illustrators to create original strips and new characters. Other publishers followed suit. In this wild swirl of competition, the comic book industry began to take shape. Since almost all the major players were Jewish, Jewish writers and illustrators were free to apply for work. This was their chance to start a career in the broader publishing trade. As Jerry and Joe worked on new characters far away in Cleveland, the delivery system for their creations was being built.

By the mid-1930s a short, dapper, well-connected, and highly successful publisher named Harry Donenfeld was contemplating entry into the emerging field. Donenfeld had an appetite for success and the track record to prove it. He knew how to pick titles that sold, hire writers with sizzle, print on the cheap, and, if necessary, muscle his magazines into newsstands, drugstores, cigar stores, barbershops, and beauty salons.

Wining and dining wealthy businessmen and powerful politicians at the best restaurants in Manhattan, he spared no expense for his potential clients, influential colleagues, and fun-loving friends.

Donenfeld had made a fortune back in the Roaring Twenties by publishing girlie magazines and racy pulp titles, which had sold as fast as his rackety printing presses could roll them out. With Prohibition in force, Donenfeld had supplemented his publishing profits by transporting stockpiles of bootleg whiskey into New York. He had hid the illegal booze in train cars carrying paper shipments from Canada and sold the hooch to speakeasies across the city, while marketing his magazines and books nationwide. Harry Donenfeld was living the high life—on his terms. His wife Gussie kept their home in the Bronx like a showplace as Donenfeld paraded his girlfriends through the glitziest clubs in town.

But those Roaring Twenties gave way to the Depression, Prohibition was repealed, and the world was far less forgiving of questionable business dealings. Political reformers were looking askance at big shots who cashed in on borderline pornography while millions of decent, out-of-work Americans scrambled to keep from starving. By 1937 New York mayor Fiorello LaGuardia was running for reelection on the promise of shutting down indecent books and magazines, and prosecutors were bringing indictments against risqué publishers. So Donenfeld set out to establish a more legitimate product line. He thought bigger and played harder than anyone else in the fledgling comic book field and figured he could get in on the ground floor and gobble up the profits. The comic book trade was still limited, but the potential for growth was promising. He needed a breakthrough title. He had no way of knowing that two young men in Cleveland had created a character who could provide that kind of breakthrough.

TO MOVE INTO THE COMIC FIELD, Donenfeld turned to his friend, business partner, and spiritual opposite Jack Liebowitz, a no-nonsense, detail-savvy accountant who had grown up in the same Lower East Side, New York, neighborhood as the flamboyant Donenfeld. In contrast to Donenfeld, during those same Roaring Twenties, Liebowitz had studied accounting at night at New York University and had gone to work as a financial manager for the International Ladies Garment Workers Union. He got by on a modest salary while working to win higher wages and better working conditions for immigrants who toiled in crowded sweatshops for 12 to 14 hours a day.

Liebowitz, whose parents had left Ukraine and settled in New York City when he was three, could relate to the hardworking garment makers and believe in their cause. But by the early 1930s, with the Depression bearing down, the striking union out of money, and radical communists attempting a takeover, Liebowitz was more than ready to go into business with a smooth operator from the old neighborhood.

So, the mild-mannered accountant and the back-slapping business tycoon cast their gaze on the emerging comic book business. As the first commercial comic books rolled off the same presses that printed cheap pulp magazines like *Ghost Stories, Strange Suicides,* and *Medical Horrors,* Donenfeld and Liebowitz maneuvered for an opening. By 1938 the pair had taken over National Allied Publications and DC Comics (publisher of *Detective Comics*), thus setting themselves up as major players in the emerging comic book industry.

Action Comics No. I introduced Superman to the world.

CHAPTER 5

CHAMPION OF THE OPPRESSED

AS THE COMIC BOOK INDUSTRY took shape in New York, Jerry and Joe were eking out a living by operating their own two-man comic business in Cleveland. The aspiring writer and illustrator were living with their parents to save on expenses, working from a makeshift studio in Joe's attic, and working menial part-time jobs to make ends meet. Having managed to get a couple of contracts with new comic book publishers in New York, the pair developed a few interesting characters. Their title *Federal Men* featured a wisecracking Federal Bureau of Investigation (FBI) agent named Steve Carson who worked undercover to find kidnapped babies and shut down criminal gangs. Spooky Dr. Occult was a brash, supernatural ghost detective who tracked down zombies, vampires, and other spectral figures. In some episodes the evil Dr. Occult even donned a red cape and took flight as the creators tried out a bit of their Superman material. As the work ebbed and flowed, Jerry and Joe waited for their big break. That's where Superman was supposed to come in.

At first Jerry insisted on holding back the Superman character from the low-paying comic book publishers in hopes of selling it to an established newspaper syndicate. A major syndicate like King Features or United Features could place a Superman strip in hundreds of newspapers nationwide and generate thousands of dollars in royalties in the process. A portion of the royalties would go to the creators week after week, month after month, year after year, for the life of the strip. Strips like *Little Orphan Annie* and *Popeye* had been popular in newspapers for years, and their creators were dining at the top of the comic-art food chain. But the strategy of saving Superman for syndication had produced only a drawer full of rejection letters from syndicate executives, who claimed that an all-powerful being from another planet, dressed in tights and serving the public good, was too far-fetched for a broad newspaper audience comprised mostly of adults. One editor from United Features indelicately summed up Superman as "a rather immature piece of work."

Losing patience with rejections, Jerry and Joe finally sent off Superman samples to comic book publishers, only to receive more negative feedback. With no one in the publishing business showing interest in the Superman character, the Man of Steel sat on the shelf. Then, one day in the spring of 1938, Jerry and Joe opened the mail to find an intriguing proposal from DC Comics—Harry Donenfeld's promising new venture. The letter came from editor Vin Sullivan, who had been assigned to launch a new title, *Action Comics (AC)*, to build on the success of DC Comics. Jerry and Joe had created a couple of the lesser characters for Donenfeld's publications, but this new one sounded bigger. Sullivan wanted a 13-page Superman adventure as the lead story for the debut issue of *AC*. Sullivan was desperate for a good character and didn't have time to start from scratch with a new concept. He had come across an old, rejected Superman proposal, and he was willing to pay Siegel and Shuster to recraft it for *AC*—pronto. Jerry and Joe's company would have to produce the four-color cover and 13 pages of illustrated text in a couple of weeks to meet a fast-approaching deadline.

Tired of watching their best character sit on the shelf as new comic books rolled out new superheroes every week (even the word "super" was turning up regularly), Siegel and Shuster accepted the offer and began scrambling to fill the order. After a series of back-and-forth rewrites, remakes, and spats between the Cleveland collaborators and the New York publishers, 200,000 copies of the comic went to press in the summer of 1938. *Action Comics* No. 1 hit the newsstands with Superman on the cover. The hero is effortlessly lifting a car as men scramble in stupefied horror.

Although the story would be embellished and refined in future editions, the first page of panels in *Action Comics* No. 1 lays out the superhero's basic origins and core identity. It also reveals his decidedly liberal leanings. Superman bursts onto the scene as the New Deal blend of optimism and social responsibility, a muscular do-gooder with a boundless passion for justice. Or as *Action Comics* No. 1 puts it:

Superman! Champion of the Oppressed. The physical marvel who has sworn to devote his existence to helping those in need.

The first page sums up the origin of Superman in a manner that would hold up for decades to come:

"As a distant planet is destroyed by old age, a scientist placed his infant son in a hastily devised space-ship, launching it toward earth." The baby is found by "a passing motorist, who, discovering the sleeping babe within, turned the child over to an orphanage." The baby amazes the orphanage staff with incredible feats of strength, "including lifting a chair over his head with one hand." Named Clark, the boy can leap 1/8 mile, hurdle a 20-story building, and outrun a train. In addition, "Nothing less than a bursting shell could penetrate his skin." Clark is driven to "turn his titanic strength into channels that would benefit mankind, and so was created 'Superman,' champion of the oppressed."

Over the next 13 pages, Superman sets out on a furious series of missions, all reflecting the ideals of democracy, compassion for the weak, hope for the future, defense of the rule of law, and respect for justice. The staccato style of the writing, the redundancies in the wording, and the hectic pace of the panels all reflect the hurried nature of the production and the relative inexperience of the creators. But despite these shortcomings, the essence of the character lived up to the hype as "the most astounding fiction character of all time." Standing for good government, general prosperity, and an equal chance for all, the Man of Steel had arrived on the scene with strength, power, and plenty of good intentions.

In one scene, Superman flies to the governor's mansion to save an innocent woman from wrongful execution. Tearing off the door to the governor's bedroom, he explains, "Evelyn Curry is to be electrocuted in 15 minutes for murder. I have proof here of her innocence, a signed confession." After the amazed governor reads the confession from the real murderer, he calls the state prison to halt the execution. Superman vanishes in a flash but leaves behind a note—and the actual murderer, bound and gagged, is on the front lawn of the governor's mansion. The governor tells his aides, "Gentlemen, I still can't believe my senses. He's not human. Thank God he is apparently on the side of law and order."

In another quick set of panels, a frantic call comes in to the newspaper office. The caller reports that a man is beating his wife. Clark races out of the office to cover the story. He arrives at the couple's apartment in his Superman outfit to find the woman lying on the floor, her abusive husband standing over her with a strap. The abuser attacks Superman with a knife, but "with a sharp snap the blade snaps on Superman's hard skin." After Superman warns, "You're going to get a lesson you'll never forget," the man faints, and the police arrive to take him away.

The early Superman adventures of 1938 also feature a story that underscores Superman's impatience with wealthy industrialists who put profit ahead of public good. In this tale Superman takes his New Deal spirit to an extreme, and a band of rich partiers almost pays the price with their lives. Superman descends into a coal mine to save a miner trapped in a cave-in. After discovering that the cave-in resulted from unsafe conditions—the owner of the mine had failed to maintain the safety equipment and an alarm signal—the Man of Steel swings into action. Rushing to the mine owner's mansion, Superman crashes a party of well-to-do socialites and promises to let the mine owner and his high-society guests "see how the other side lives." Then he leads them all into the mine.

Deep below the Earth's surface, the socialites twirl their pearl necklaces, fiddle with their top hats, and express their astonishment that "people actually work down here." Then Superman pulls down a beam that supports the mine walls, which causes another cave-in and traps the partiers in an underground hole. Since the emergency alarm doesn't work, the trapped socialites have no choice but to dig their way out: "Knee deep in stagnant water, struggling with unwieldy tools, slipping, frequently falling, the entrapped pleasure-seekers seek desperately...to batter down the huge barrier of coal." In the end the mine owner vows to run the "safest mine in America," and Superman rescues the party.

The debut issue also introduces Lois Lane and sets up her complex relationship with Clark and Superman. Lois, a strong woman working in a man's world, knows exactly what she likes. She likes the supremely confident, splendidly sculpted, all-powerful Superman. She merely tolerates the meek and squeamish Clark Kent.

The final lines of the Superman adventure in *Action Comics* No. 1 urge readers to look for more in the future:

And so begins the startling adventures of the most sensational strip character of all time.

SUPERMAN!

A physical marvel. A mental wonder. Superman is destined to reshape the destiny of the world.

The entire print run of *Action Comics* No. 1 sold out, and Siegel and Shuster were commissioned to generate more content. Toward the end of 1938 it was clear: The Man of Steel was a hit. Customers were asking for the next installment of Superman rather than the next edition of *Action Comics*.

By the end of 1938 the print run exceeded one million, and sales topped $11 million. In episode after episode the Man of Steel defends democracy; sticks up for the oppressed; and thwarts criminals, corrupt politicians, and greedy industrialists. Siegel and Shuster's character was raw, rough, tough, and unpredictable. At times he threatened his adversaries with serious injury—even death—for failing to follow his commands. One of his favorite tactics was to grab an adversary by the scruff of the neck, fly him thousands of feet into the sky, and threaten to let him fall to a certain death unless he confessed or incriminated others. Superman distrusted government authority and reveled in bringing extravagant wealth and privileged arrogance to justice. He showed a concern for international affairs, and his exploits often transcended national borders. He was the champion of oppressed people everywhere and would often fly to South America to stop brutal dictators from exploiting the masses. This superhero—the first to become an icon of modern pop culture—knew few limits. In some episodes, the creators let Superman's Jewish roots slip out. *Action Comics* No. 7 opens with this line: "Friend of the helpless and oppressed is Superman, a man possessing the strength of a dozen Samsons."

For Jerry and Joe it was a dream come true. They had their names on a wildly popular comic book, were earning excellent wages, and were part of the big-time publishing scene in New York City. Sure, they had relinquished the copyright to DC Comics but that was standard operating procedure at the time. Looking ahead to the future, wondering about the possibilities of this fantastic character, they felt the sky was the limit.

PART TWO

EMERGING FROM THE SHADOWS

The Ku Klux Klan was shrouded in mystery. The robed and hooded vigilantes held bizarre rituals in the dead of night, in the light of their emblematic burning cross. The organization's Imperial Wizards and Grand Dragons appealed to white protestant men to rise up against Jews, Negroes, immigrants, and their supporters. Tapping in to fear and ignorance, the KKK promised its followers that America could be ruled by one race, one religion, and one color. In the rural South, an iconoclastic young man was getting a first-hand education in the ways of the Klan. He would go on to try to tear off the mask of the secret society.

During the Great Depression poverty gripped much of the rural South, as evidenced by this family of migrant workers outside a citrus packing plant in Winter Haven, Florida.

CHAPTER 6

ORANGE GROVES & HOODED HORSES

SEVEN-YEAR-OLD Stetson Kennedy took a seat on the curb on Main Street in downtown Jacksonville, Florida. The air was warm, the crowd was festive, and the parade was about to begin. Crooking his neck for a better view, he immediately became engrossed in the spectacle. First came a row of men wearing white robes and hoods and mounted on great white stallions. Even the horses were bedecked with flowing saddle covers and ornamental hoods. When the riders pulled on the reins, the steeds rose up on their hind legs, whinnied, snorted, and furiously pawed the air. Following the riders were dozens of robed and hooded men marching four or five abreast. As Kennedy recalls, "One of the mounted knights of the KKK bore a flaming fiery cross, while the other blew long, mournful blasts on a bugle." Kennedy was awestruck. This was his introduction to the Ku Klux Klan.

Kennedy was born in Jacksonville, Florida, in 1916. He grew up in the 14-room, white-columned house owned by his traditional southern family. The Kennedys boasted blood ties to Confederate war heroes and wealthy cotton planters and prided themselves on carrying on the southern way of life. Kennedy's mother taught her children traditional values and manners and dutifully attended meetings of the United Daughters of the Confederacy. His father ran a furniture store and served as chairman of the board of deacons at the First Baptist Church of Jacksonville. Insatiably curious, energetic, and sensitive as a boy, Kennedy earned a reputation as the free spirit of the family. His grandmother used to offer him two cents to sit still for two minutes and almost never had to pay him the pennies.

The oldest of five children, Kennedy spent much of his free time exploring the surrounding woods, creeks, orchards, and orange groves. He loved to write stories and poems about the birds, animals, trees, and waterways that defined rural North Florida. In time he began to contemplate the lives of the people who lived on the ramshackle farms and in the small towns in the area. Sensing an injustice in the poverty that gripped the lives of so many, he began to feel a burning passion to do something about it. He was particularly disturbed by the prevailing view that "colored folk" were to be treated as subservient to white people. Although he couldn't quite understand why, that pervasive racism got under his skin. "It happened early," Kennedy would recall later in his life. "Whatever *it* was." Still, he saw his family as "no more, no less, racist than the norm, par for the course, southern white."

Shortly after attending that Ku Klux Klan parade, Kennedy began to see the truth about the men in hoods and robes. He had thought the KKK was a club for grown-ups who got to dress up in Halloween costumes year-round until his mother told him that the organization actually kept the folks in "colored town" in line. But his real lesson occurred at the bedside of his family's African-American housekeeper, whom Klansmen had beaten for the offense of talking back to a white streetcar operator who had shortchanged her. Hearing the woman describe the brutal attack, Kennedy realized that the men behind the masks were bullies who terrorized innocent black people. He began to detest the ingrained racism that infected the world around him and to feel out of step with those who accepted it. "I've always felt like an alien in the land of my birth," he recalled later.

At Robert E. Lee High School in Jacksonville, Kennedy's attitude toward race made him as much an outsider as Jerry Siegel and Joe Shuster were hundreds of miles away at Glenville High. Kennedy refused to play along with classmates who taunted their colored servants or knocked black newspaper boys off their bikes for fun.

"What's up with Stet?" his friends would ask.

"What's up with all of you?" Kennedy thought. Confused by the pervasive antiblack attitudes, he found little support from other white kids.

At the dinner table one of his three sisters once said, "I do believe you'd rather be with niggers than with us."

Kennedy replied, "As a matter of fact, I would." He then got up and stomped out of the room. The white adults around him shared the view that blacks were inferior to whites—particularly the uncle who kept a hood and robe in his closet.

As a young man Kennedy worked at his father's furniture store in hopes of using his earnings to see the world or to attend college. As part of his job he traveled from door to door and farm to farm to collect payments on furniture that had been sold for "a dollar down and a dollar a week." Sitting with poor white and black men and women struggling to put food on the table, he often put away the payment book, took out a notebook, and drew out the stories of their fascinating lives and daunting hardships. While Jerry and Joe were surrounding themselves with stories of space travelers and wise-cracking detectives, Kennedy was immersing himself in stories of former slaves and tenant farmers. While Jerry and Joe were dreaming up a superhero to protect regular people, Kennedy was beginning to think about becoming a writer too—but the kind of writer who would tell the stories of regular people in order to help them with real problems.

In 1936 Kennedy enrolled at the University of Florida and spent a year studying history and writing. He became more articulate about his critique of racism in the Deep South and the rest of the country. He recalls thinking, "Don't ask me what was wrong with me. What was wrong with the rest of the state, and South, and nation, and world, that was engaged in that sort of oppression of one people over another?"

After only a year at the university Kennedy's headstrong ambition and restless spirit propelled him faster than classes, papers, and exams would allow. He placed a load of books on a boat and shipped them off to Key West. He then hitchhiked down to the Keys, caught up with the books, married a local girl, and began a job as a junior interviewer with the Works Progress Administration Florida Writers' Project, a New Deal program that provided work to unemployed writers, editors, historians, and researchers.

The writers' task was to record the life stories, tall tales, folk songs, and fables of ordinary people. They used a clumsy recording machine with a sapphire needle that cut sound directly onto a 12-inch acetate disc. Kennedy recalls, "We traveled backroads the length and breadth of the

Florida peninsula, toting a coffee-table-sized recording machine into turpentine camps, sawmills, citrus groves, the Everglades, out onto railroad tracks, and aboard shrimp trawlers—wherever Florida folks were working, living, and singing." By age 21, Kennedy was earning $37.50 every two weeks and felt like "a kid on a treasure hunt."

Within a year Kennedy was leading a team of story and song gatherers on expeditions across the state. He gained a deep understanding of how folktales, songs, and rituals form the glue that holds society together. At one stop, while setting up the recording machine to capture folk songs from a group of black singers, he was surprised when one woman broke into prayer. "Dear Lord, this is Eartha White talkin' to you again," that recording begins. "I just want to thank you for giving mankind the intelligence to make such a marvelous machine, and a president like Franklin D. Roosevelt who cares about preserving the songs people sing."

In his travels Kennedy was particularly moved by his visits to turpentine camps—squalid encampments set deep in the woods where black workers stripped the bark off pine trees and drained the sap into buckets to make turpentine. The camp hands worked dreadfully long hours, and the company docked their paychecks for the privilege of eating its cornmeal mush and sleeping in its grim shanties, which resembled the ramshackle huts that slaves once occupied. This arrangement placed the workers in constant debt to the company, which held them as virtual prisoners constantly working to try to pay off their debt. Kennedy asked one elderly worker, "Why don't you leave and get out of it?"

The man responded, "The onliest way out is to die out."

As Kennedy captured the stories of turpentine campers, Native American healers, and shantytown fishermen, Jerry and Joe were churning out the first panels of Superman a thousand miles away in Cleveland. As Kennedy recorded blues songs of poor black field hands, Jerry and Joe produced images of Superman collaring hoodlums and saving Lois Lane.

IN 1940 STETSON KENNEDY left his folklore-collecting job. He planned to concentrate more on his writing. He could use the information and insight gained from his childhood encounters with the poor, his studies at the university, and his experience as a folklorist to expose deep-seated racism and the threat posed by the Ku Klux Klan. As a folklorist Kennedy knew that the Klan used its invented rituals, concocted language, and biased belief system to imbue otherwise weak men with a sense of mastery and power. Kennedy knew the typical Klansman felt like a bigger man after taking part in mysterious rituals, speaking in a secret language, or attacking people judged to be inferior. Kennedy wanted to sweep away the mystique—to show the Klan as nothing more than a violent hate group selling a fantasy of the past. He wanted to expose the KKK's false premises, bogus beliefs, secrets, and fake mysticism and to let ridicule, rejection, and scorn "melt the cultural glue" that held the club together. "The main idea was to make bigotry obnoxious." He attacked the Klan with confidence and zeal.

Naturally Kennedy was just a person and had no superpowers, but he was well aware of the power of words. His friend and frequent houseguest Woody Guthrie—the famed folksinger who wrote "This Land Is Your Land"—often used a one-line answer to friends who asked, "Where's Stet?" Guthrie would reply that Kennedy was making more ammo with his typewriter upstairs in the attic.

Using that ammo, Kennedy embarked on a campaign to correct the historic and journalistic record of the KKK. He told himself to write as much as possible, focusing on exposés that revealed the real inner workings of the Klan. More newspaper articles. His pieces countered those of mainstream journalists who described KKK ceremonies with such terms as "mystic," "eerie," and "awesome." More magazine articles. He criticized journalists who presented the KKK side of the story as a valid point of view in the contemporary political debate. More exposés. He criticized respected encyclopedias that described the secret order as a legitimate political organization comprised of white protestant men dedicated to protecting the white Christian race from the threat of Negro uprising, Jewish dominance, and widespread immorality. He knew the Klan would fight back. After all, it had been silencing its critics for a long time.

The Civil War was fought mostly in the South, and the devastation that remained served as a constant reminder to southerners that they had lost the war.

CHAPTER 7

THE ORIGINAL KLAN

OVER THE YEARS historians have contended that the original Ku Klux Klan was a joke. Literally. Drawn mainly from the work of southern writers who were close to the secret society's founders and often repeated to this day, the story goes like this: The original Klan began as a social club for a handful of men with time on their hands, a taste for the absurd, and a penchant for harmless mischief. In the spring of 1866, in the town of Pulaski, Tennessee, a half dozen men met at the office of a prominent attorney to dream up a diversion from the doldrums of small-town life.

Just back from the Civil War with no immediate plans for the future, the former Confederate officers decided to form a social society much like the student fraternities gaining popularity on college campuses. The founders struggled to come up with a name until one man threw out the word *kuklos*—Greek for "circle" or "band." His fellow brainstormers quickly added the word "clan" but started it with a *K* to harden the alliteration and to add a touch of mystery. After a bit of back and forth the founders had their name: Ku Klux Klan. They liked the sound of it. It felt like bones rattling in the closet.

Building on the mysterious name, the "circle of brothers" added weird wardrobes, unusual rituals, mysterious code words, and absolute secrecy to the group. Members were required to wear handmade robes that flowed to the floor and high, pointed hoods that added two or three feet to their height. The officers were given titles drawn from mythology or just made up on the spot. The chief officer was the Grand Cyclops, his assistant was the Grand Magi, and the rank and file were Ghouls.

After outgrowing their original meeting place, as local lore has it, the Klan moved to a more alluring venue: the ruins of an old farmhouse that had been decimated by a storm, engulfed with fallen trees, and rumored to be haunted. In strange midnight ceremonies the men donned their ghostly garb, recited their rambling incantations, pledged vows of secrecy, and indoctrinated new recruits. In time, the robed and hooded figures, masquerading as ghosts of Confederate soldiers returning from the battle-field, mounted horses and rode through neighboring farms and villages. The ghastly, ghostly figures told shocked onlookers that they had not had a drink since the Battle of Shiloh and had rode twice around the world since suppertime. Soon dozens of new dens had formed throughout the region, and sightings of hooded night riders were commonplace. Major newspapers speculated that this mysterious secret order must have a greater mission—for good or evil.

BY THE BEGINNING OF 1867, with the movement spreading beyond the control of its founders, the first Klansmen invited all known dens to a secret convention in Nashville to elect a leader, to draft a constitution, and to set a course for the future. The convention elected former Confederate general Nathan Bedford Forrest as Grand Wizard (supreme leader) and designated the entire South as the territory of the new Invisible Empire. The empire was divided into realms that generally corresponded with states, dominions that corresponded with congressional districts, and dens that would serve as local chapters. Former military officers were bestowed with such titles as Grand Dragon, Grand Titan, and Grand Giant, and the rank and file remained the Ghouls. The Klan constitution—or prescript—expressed allegiance to the U.S. government but also asserted the power to interpret and enforce the law. In effect this declaration made the KKK judge, jury, and executioner of its own version of law and order.

KKK leaders also positioned the organization as the front line of opposition to Reconstruction, the federal effort to repair the damage caused by the Civil War. The South had just lost the war, and the vast majority of white Southerners were furious about the new Reconstruction Act of 1868, which mandated northern military occupation of much of the South, invalidated most of the region's state governments, and decreed that the rights of newly freed slaves would be guaranteed—by force if necessary. The opponents of Reconstruction dubbed the northern intruders as carpetbaggers, their southern supporters as scalawags, and African Americans as inferiors. They vowed to resist what they saw as the unfair trampling of their rights. The KKK would become their army.

In the weeks after the convention General Forrest's old soldiers transformed themselves into terrorists, forming paramilitary units to wage a guerrilla war against carpetbaggers, scalawags, and Negroes. Cloaked in white robes and hoods and armed with rifles, whips, and swords, the ex-Rebel troops took their places as the foot soldiers of the KKK. The Ghouls set out on raiding parties that targeted supporters of Reconstruction, white or black. They lashed white teachers at Negro schools with bullwhips and burned their schoolhouses to the ground. Freed slaves who spoke out for equality were dragged from their homes and beaten—even burned—in front of their children. Black men charged with crimes were broken out of jail and hanged in plain view without a trial. In remote areas raiders tarred and feathered their victims. Once the tar cooled it stuck to the victim's skin, and removing it left survivors scarred for life.

Many newspapers characterized the raids as acts of self-defense on behalf of the entire white race. The apologists of the Klan recast its atrocities as heroics and spread fanciful myths about its origin and purpose. For example, most white Southerners believed that the club chose the name Ku Klux Klan not because of its mysterious sound but because it simulated the sound of cocking and discharging a firearm.

By 1870 KKK atrocities had grown so extreme that editors of respected newspapers were denouncing the violence and national political leaders were demanding an end to it. In the South prominent citizens began dropping out of the organization—although common thugs filled their places and used the robes and hoods as cover for crimes ranging from chicken theft to bank robbery. Fearful of being prosecuted, General Forrest finally declared that the organization had been "perverted" and ordered his followers to stand down. He ordered that hoods and masks be burned, records be destroyed, and night-riding violence be halted. A few heeded the call. Most did not. In the end Congress launched a massive investigation, filling 11 volumes with evidence of an unprecedented reign of floggings, beatings, burnings, shootings, hangings, and torture over a four-year span. In 1872 Congress passed a law allowing Klansmen to be tried in federal court, and government troops moved in to mop up the diehards.

By the mid-1880s the Klan was mostly gone—but so were the carpetbaggers and scalawags. The Reconstruction program, mired in scandal, steeped in controversy, and exhausted by struggle, was largely abandoned. The federal government let the South deal with its own problems. The old white ruling class regained power and restored white supremacy as the rule of law. Black people were essentially denied the vote, forced into servitude, and persecuted for even questioning the system. Historians generally glossed over the old KKK atrocities, while southern novelists romanticized them with elaborate tales of a valiant masked and hooded army that rode at night to save the downtrodden white race from the dual horrors of northern tyranny and black rule. As the nation moved toward a new century, the Klan remained much as it had started—shrouded in mystery.

The highly controversial film *The Birth of a Nation* used breakthrough cinematic techniques to glorify the original Ku Klux Klan.

CHAPTER 8

BACK FROM THE DEAD

THE PRIME MOVER of the next rising of the KKK was William J. Simmons, the son of a Civil War veteran from the Deep South. His father had ridden with the original night riders during Reconstruction. As a boy growing up on his family's farm in the hamlet of Harpersville, Alabama, Simmons first heard the romanticized accounts of valiant, hooded night riders and saw the fear in the eyes of black servants and field hands who had felt their wrath.

As a young man Simmons left the farm, served an undistinguished tour of duty in the Spanish-American War, and returned home to make his mark. He trained to be a minister and took to the preaching circuit, only to be drummed out of the Southern Methodist Episcopal Church for "ineffectiveness and moral failings." Still searching for a life path, Simmons moved to Atlanta, Georgia, and found work as a salesman and college lecturer before taking a job promoting fraternal organizations much like today's Elks, Masons, and Shriners. Rising to the rank of colonel in the Woodmen of the World, Simmons proudly told friends and associates that he was now a professional "fraternalist"—and he dreamed of resurrecting the fraternity of the KKK.

In the spring of 1915—just about the time Jerry Siegel, Joe Shuster, and Stetson Kennedy were born—a twist of fate gave Simmons the time he needed to plan the resurgence. After being injured in a car accident, Simmons spent a three-month recuperation period remaking the secret order as a modern association of white, native-born, protestant men. He saw nostalgia, romance, and dollar signs in the prospect and threw himself into the task.

Simmons tracked down a copy of the original Klan Prescript and repackaged it as a 54-page, novel-size handbook entitled *The Kloran*. He embellished the standard white robe and redesigned the hood to be less showy and more menacing, down to two narrow slits for the eyes. He reworded the membership oath, revised the initiation ceremony, devised hand signs and code words, restored old titles, and devised new ones. He began concocting a language that emphasized the infamous *K* sound. The local meeting place became the Klavern, the regional convention became the Klonvocation, and the art of being a Klansman became Klancraft.

The new Klan would charge $10 for membership and $6.50 for a cheap robe and hood, and it would even offer optional life insurance policies. Finally, with the flair of an artist, the diminutive promoter added the pièce de résistance—the final flourish. Borrowing a literary device from the pro-Klan novel *The Clansman,* he created a central role for the burning cross. The original Klan had not used the flaming cross, but it would become the ever-present, fiery symbol of the new one.

After lining up more than a dozen influential men to serve in the upper ranks, Simmons copyrighted his enhancements and secured an official charter from the state of Georgia. The new Invisible Empire of the Knights of the Ku Klux Klan was established as a benevolent, nonprofit, fraternal organization—at first more of a force for uniting white protestant men than for attacking their perceived enemies. With the pieces in place, the founder—now known as the Little Colonel—set out to dramatize the mystery of his restored empire.

On the eve of Thanksgiving 1915, Simmons invited a group of his influential friends to a meeting at the Piedmont Hotel in Atlanta. Afterward, 16 believers climbed into a tour bus and set out on an eight-mile drive to Stone Mountain, a slab of pure granite that climbs 800 feet above the surrounding area. Brandishing flashlights, the expedition party made its way to a ledge near the summit. There, as a cold night wind whipped, the robed and hooded men built a makeshift altar from flagstones, draped it with an American flag, and decorated it with a Bible, a canteen of baptismal water, and a sword. Simmons and his followers erected a rag-covered wooden cross, doused it with kerosene, and set it ablaze. In the light of the ceremonial fire the Ku Klux Klan was called back from the dead.

THE CEREMONY on Stone Mountain reawakened the sleeping giant. Now it was time to fire up the masses. Simmons had that figured out too. He planned the public announcement to coincide with the Atlanta premier of *The Birth of a Nation,* a two-hour silent-film spectacular set in the South during the tumultuous aftermath of the Civil War. Filmmaker D. W. Griffith had used state-of-the-art cinematic techniques to drive home his controversial message that white vigilantes had saved decent white families. Simmons reserved space for ads introducing "The Greatest

Fraternal Organization on Earth" adjacent to the movie promotions in the *Atlanta Constitution*. Then he waited.

On December 6, 1915, at 8 p.m.—two weeks after the Stone Mountain ritual—*The Birth of a Nation* debuted to a standing-room crowd at the majestic, red-carpeted Atlanta Theater. The love scenes were presented in dramatic close-ups. The epic battle scenes appeared in sweeping panorama. A 30-piece orchestra performed a swelling musical score. The audience was spellbound. A graying Civil War veteran wiped a tear as the camera scanned the desolate, smoldering wasteland of his defeated homeland. A middle-age woman cringed as a band of lustful, ravenous Negroes clawed at the door of a remote cabin in pursuit of an innocent, terrified white girl. A teenage boy slapped the back of a man in front of him as a bugle blast rose from the orchestra pit and a long line of hooded riders thundered onto the screen, their path illuminated by a burning cross.

The entire audience cheered as the Ku Klux Klan rode to the rescue of white womanhood, white power, and white supremacy. Finally the crowd breathed a final sigh of relief as the robed avengers dispensed with the threat by castrating and lynching the black villain. And the show did not end with the final scene. As the audience filed out of the theater, a bonus scene awaited them on Peachtree Street. More than a hundred men in white robes and hoods stood in military-style formation, rifles raised into the air. Thanks to the Little Colonel, the Ku Klux Klan was back— and this was no movie.

In the 1920s the Ku Klux Klan displayed its political clout by staging massive marches in the nation's capital.

CHAPTER 9

A BOLD NEW MESSAGE

IN THE SPRING OF 1920 Simmons walked into the offices of the Southern Publicity Association in Atlanta. The leaders of this pioneering firm had built its reputation by devising successful publicity and fund-raising programs for clients ranging from the Anti-Saloon League to the Red Cross. The firm's inseparable male and female partners were also becoming known for their creativity, connections, and can-do spirit—even if their close personal relationship was raising eyebrows.

Bessie Tyler provided the passion for the company. She stood close to six feet tall, swore like a sailor, and usually dressed in black, from her patent-leather pumps to her broad, flowing cape. Tyler knew how to make people sit up and take notice—and how to turn adversity into advantage. Her partner was Edward Young Clarke, the business brains of the outfit. Clarke was a spin doctor before the term existed, a master of deception who never let the truth get in the way of his clients' needs. Clarke knew how to turn negative publicity into positive headlines—and how to turn controversy into cash.

After hearing out Simmons, Tyler and Clarke made a round of calls to newspaper and magazine editors across the country to test the waters. To their happy astonishment, most of the newsmen were more than open to running stories about the new Ku Klux Klan. Even better for the publicity mavens, the interest from the press was not limited to the South. Editors from the Northeast, Midwest, and West Coast asked for regular releases about the revived Klan too. Tyler and Clarke were confident that a bold new message—coupled with an aggressive membership campaign—could drive growth nationwide. Their challenge was to make the job lucrative enough for themselves—particularly since going to work for the Klan would mean the loss of their Jewish clientele. Over a two-week period in 1920, Tyler and Clarke worked out an astounding contract with Simmons. The public relations duo would get four of every five dollars in new membership fees plus profits from merchandise sales for the life of the campaign. Seeing dollar signs, Tyler and Clarke went to work.

THE FIRST STEP was to refocus the Klan's message for the modern world. It was the aftermath of World War I, and change was in the air. Immigrants were pouring into the country and taking good jobs at low wages. Women had won the vote and were demanding more influence in public affairs. Black men were mustering out of the military and pressing for equality in their own country. Morals were changing too, as the focus of American life shifted from the small town to the city. Young people flocked to nightclubs and speakeasies, whiskey flowed like water, jazz played on the radio, and divorce became more of an option for unhappy couples. Many white men feared that their traditional place atop the social order—even their status as heads of their own households—was endangered. The Klan had to speak to those people and tap into their fear.

So, to the well-known goal of stamping down blacks and Jews, Tyler and Clarke added new targets: Catholics, Asians, Mexicans, labor unionists, socialists, and greedy Wall Street tycoons. To the Klan's historic opposition to racial integration and religious tolerance, they added the evils of dope, booze, sex, corruption, nightclubs, roadhouses, and violations of the Sabbath. Seeking to differentiate the Klan from other fraternal organizations, they positioned it as the most militant enforcer of morality and decency in communities across the country. Then they pushed the new message through the media.

The PR team persuaded newsreel producers to make short, pro-Klan films for movie theaters. They hired a Chicago advertising agency to design newspaper ads and billboards and placed them coast-to-coast. They organized elaborate Klan ceremonies, speeches, and rallies that drew hundreds of new recruits and thousands of onlookers.

Tyler coached Simmons to talk less about white brotherhood and more about black inferiority, Jewish greed, and the plans of the Roman Catholic Church to dominate America. Simmons delivered the expanded message in interviews with major newspapers and in crowded meeting halls full of potential members. At one event he stepped forward to deliver his message to a group of influential men who could serve in important roles in his organization. Standing behind a bare table in the front of the room, Simmons at first said nothing. Then he placed his Colt automatic on the table. Then he placed his revolver on the table. Then he placed his ammunition belt on the table. Then he plunged his bowie knife into the tabletop. Then he said, "Now let the Niggers, Catholics, [and] Jews . . . come on."

THE TACTICS PROVED a stunning success. A year into the campaign, more than 100,000 men had paid their ten-dollar Klecktoken (initiation fee)—and all the takings were tax-free because the KKK was chartered as a charitable organization. Traveling promoters called Kleagles were offered a cut of the dues to sign up new members. Driven more by the money than the message, most Kleagles targeted any white protestant man willing to part with ten dollars. As one journalist put it, the prospect list included "the poor, the romantic, the short-witted, the bored, the vindictive, the bigoted and the ambitious."

As dues poured into Klan bank accounts, merchandise poured out of its warehouses. The new mandate was sell, sell, sell. The product line included more than 40 newsletters, bottles of initiation water, and a pocketknife—"a 100-percent knife for 100 percent Americans." Sell more! For the romantic Klansman there was even a gift for the wife or girlfriend: a jewel-studded pendant in the form of a fiery cross. Sell more! The demand for robes and hoods became so great that a dedicated robe factory had to be set up in Atlanta to fill the orders. Sell more! Within a few short years of the Tyler-Clarke campaign, more than four million Americans had joined the KKK, and revenues topped $75 million. Despite the success, Simmons would soon be ousted in a contentious coup led by his number two man, Hiram Evans. In exchange for grudgingly turning the organization over to Evans, Simmons retired with a $146,500 buy-out and a house dubbed Klan Krest. Now that the Klan had the muscle of a huge membership and vast income, Evans wanted to make the organization more than just a hate-mongering money machine. By staking out positions on political issues and placing Klansmen in government offices, the KKK could become a political powerhouse. In August 1925, 40,000 Klansmen marched down Pennsylvania Avenue in Washington, D.C., as a show of strength during the Democratic National Convention. By then the KKK controlled dozens of mayors, judges, police chiefs, state legislators, congressmen, and senators.

Surprisingly, the biggest growth of the KKK did not occur in the South. The smooth-talking Grand Dragon of the Realm of Indiana, David Curtis Stephenson, built membership in his state to more than 450,000, and the organization tapped him to recruit new followers in 20 other states. Stephenson increased the ranks to more than 300,000 in neighboring Ohio, where he owned a vacation home on Buckeye Lake in rural Licking County. More than 75,000 people turned out to hear him speak at a KKK Konklave on the lake in 1923, and an equal number came back for the 1925 gathering. The Klavern in Akron, Ohio, claimed 52,000 members, making it the largest local chapter in the country. This meant that at age ten, Jerry Siegel and Joe Shuster—sheltered from any direct contact with the Klan in peaceful Glenville—were nevertheless living in proximity to tens of thousands of dedicated Klansmen.

By expanding the ranks of the Invisible Empire in the Midwest, Stephenson amassed a personal fortune of more than $3 million from his cut of dues and merchandise sales. In short order he owned a lavish mansion outside Indianapolis, a yacht on Lake Michigan, a private railroad car, and an airplane. Backed by his own private police force—the Horse Thief Detective Association—Stephenson virtually took control of Indiana's state government. "I am the law in Indiana," he liked to brag. In his public speeches he defended Prohibition and the sanctity of womanhood. In private he was an alcoholic and a womanizer.

BUT THE WEALTHY ORGANIZERS at the top had a problem. Rank-and-file members in cities and towns across the country were taking the vicious, antiblack, anti-Jewish, anti-Catholic rhetoric to heart. As had happened during the first rising of the Klan after the Civil War, violence was drawing negative attention to the organization. Klan raiding parties flogged black political candidates in North Carolina, harassed Jewish businessmen in New Jersey, attacked Catholics in Oregon, and used acid to burn the initials KKK into the foreheads of victims in Texas. And not all the victims were black, brown, Jewish, or Catholic. KKK members also targeted white protestant families for alleged immoral behavior or supposedly betraying their race or gender. In Alabama perpetrators flogged a white divorcée with two children for the crime of remarrying. In Oklahoma Ghouls lashed teenage girls for riding in cars with young men. When newspapers exposed the violence, public support began to wane. Political leaders condemned the attacks, and antimask laws went on the books to deter hooded gatherings. By the late 1920s Klan membership was falling as fast as it had risen.

But the kiss of death proved to be the hypocrisy of their leadership. Newspapers were having a field day with stories of the duplicity. After all, how could a fraternal organization that stood for law and order resort to vigilante violence? How could a handful of promoters become rich while the rank and file worked for nothing? How could people with questionable morals run a militant enforcer of strict morality? That question arose following news accounts of sexual escapades by Klan leaders. Even the intrepid Clarke and Tyler, the PR duo who had sparked the membership spike, made salacious headlines. The two were arrested—with alcohol on their breath and their clothes on the floor—in a suspected house of prostitution.

The most infamous sex scandal involved the high-flying Grand Dragon in Indiana, David Curtis Stephenson, who had not responded well to a young woman's rejection of his marriage proposal. Stephenson had his thugs kidnap the woman from her home and deliver her to his waiting train. As the train sped toward his hideaway in Chicago, Stephenson viciously beat, raped, and mauled her. Then his henchmen took her, near death, back home to Indianapolis. Two weeks later, the battered woman died from an overdose of pills, and Stephenson was charged with murder. In a highly publicized trial he was found guilty and sentenced to life in prison. KKK membership went into a nose dive.

PART THREE

JUGGERNAUT

By 1939 the Great Depression was showing signs of easing up and America was ready for a new day. Great movies like *The Wizard of Oz* and *Gone with the Wind* were drawing crowds to the theaters, jazz was pouring out of radios, and nylon stockings were all the rage for women. Preferring to remain neutral on the subject of war, most Americans didn't even want to think about the troubles in Europe. Business was ready to boom, and Superman was ready to soar. In due time German troops and tanks would roll over Austria and Poland, and the German Luftwaffe would rain bombs on London and South Hampton. As the United States began facing up to a war it had hoped to avoid, the creators of Superman began preparing for battle too.

SUPERMAN

10¢

Superman magazine debuted in the summer of 1939. It was the first comic book dedicated to an individual character.

ALL IN FULL COLOR

THE COMPLETE STORY OF THE DARING EXPLOITS OF THE ONE AND ONLY SUPERMAN

CHAPTER 10

THE BIG BLUE MONEY MACHINE

THE SUPERMAN CHARACTER was growing by leaps and bounds. In the summer of 1939, *Superman* No. 1 hit the newsstands as the first stand-alone comic book devoted to a single character. This feat was followed by the launch of the "Superman" newspaper strip, which provided the hero's growing legion of fans with daily adventures and a more complete picture of his origins on Krypton and his mission on Earth. Despite these successes, the new print products were just the beginning. An ambitious young man named Robert Maxwell Joffe was about to help make Superman a thriving business in the modern world.

Born around 1908 Robert Joffe grew up in middle-class comfort in one of the boroughs of New York City. In time his family did well enough to move from their home in a Jewish enclave of Brooklyn to a series of bigger and better houses in more affluent communities in Bedford-Stuyvesant and Flatbush. Bob's parents had thrived in those comfortable neighborhoods, far from the brutal government programs that had led to the oppression, imprisonment, or even death of tens of thousands of Jews back in the Joffes' native Russia. Bob's father had attended New York's Hebrew Technical Institute and the New York College of Dentistry and had gone on to establish his own practice. His income was high enough that he began thinking about giving something back to the world that had given him so much. While he wholeheartedly embraced the opportunities he found in America, he also clung to the traditional Jewish culture of his forebears, including the mandates to serve the broader community and to repair a broken world. He set up free dental clinics to care for children in poor neighborhoods and supported community organizations that provided health care to the needy. Bob's mother took care of the three children as she raised money for charities and volunteered for community organizations.

Bob himself had little problem juggling the twin imperatives of honoring the old culture and embracing the new. He craved the new. Like many of the sons and daughters of first-generation immigrants, he was ready to embrace the fast-paced, sky's-the-limit opportunities of New York City. In the shadows of Manhattan, his life had been one long lesson in change, and he had learned it was usually for the best. Modern synagogue centers with basketball courts and swimming pools were built on streets where ragtag kids once played kick the can. Pleasant single-family homes with front porches and green lawns sat on lots where old tenements once housed gaggles of immigrants who didn't speak English.

In the new, upscale communities Bob came to live in, kids from all backgrounds went shopping or embarked on day trips to the beach together. As a teen Joffe listened with one ear to his parents' stories of life in the old country and with the other to big band music on the radio. Like Jerry Siegel and Stetson Kennedy, Bob imagined the possibility of becoming a writer. Close to the gleaming office towers of New York, he looked

CHAMPION OF THE OPPRESSED

SUPERMAN was introduced to the world in 1938 as the Champion of the Oppressed. In time his moniker morphed into the defender of Truth, Justice, and the American Way. In his journey through comic books, comic strips, radio and TV programs, movies, and more, the character has kept a careful watch over the less fortunate and the downtrodden. From defending coal miners against unsafe working conditions (1938) to supporting protesters opposing the oppressive regime in Iran (2011), Superman has maintained a social conscience that is as strong as steel.

MANY FACES OF
SUPERMAN

FOLLOWING THE BLUEPRINT laid down by Jerry Siegel and Joe Shuster, a continuous stream of artists contributed to the evolution of Superman's character. Over the years, comic-book illustrators, TV producers, moviemakers, and digital designers have constantly modernized the look and feel of the character and his surroundings. Given the continued success of the Superman enterprise, this process seems certain to continue for years—if not generations—to come.

SWIMMING TOWARD a German U-boat. Riding a missile toward a Japanese target. Conducting special missions on the front lines. Tying cannon barrels into knots. Superman served as a stalwart supporter of the troops during World War II and in all the wars that followed. Even more important, Superman comic books provide overseas troops with much-needed relief from the stresses of war.

SUPERMAN
IN WARTIME

SPINOFF
SUPERHEROES

THE SUCCESS OF SUPERMAN spawned the creation of new comic-book superheroes. From Batman and Robin to Wonder Woman, these exciting new characters thrilled increasing numbers of readers with their amazing powers and heroic deeds. As the comic-book industry grew, stories of violent criminals and bloodthirsty vampires began crowding the newsstands. All the "blood and thunder" provided ample fodder for comic-book critics, who eventually forced the industry to impose a rigid censorship code.

out at the opportunities of the publishing industry and entertainment business. Driven by ambition that could be mistaken for arrogance, he wanted a bite of the Big Apple.

In his early 20s Bob was living at home and working as a writer, although his prose might not have met the approval of his respectable parents. He had started out with plans of becoming a songwriter but ended up churning out risqué romance novels, gritty detective stories, and blood-and-guts murder tomes for publishers in New York. Writing under the pen names Bob Maxwell, Jack Keene, and even Claire Kennedy, he learned to write fast, with sizzle and intensity, and to give the publisher exactly what he wanted: a book that would sell. His biggest client was the backslapping, money-making Harry Donenfeld, who considered Bob one of the best "smooch" writers in his stable. Donenfeld admired Bob's lurid fiction—packed with action, tinted with sex, and punctuated with violence. Some people may have written Bob off as a bottom-feeding pulp hack, but Donenfeld knew talent and saw it in his promising protégée.

In fact, Donenfeld saw the young, ambitious, well-spoken young man as more than a writer. Convinced that Bob could succeed on the business side of the publishing game, Donenfeld gave him a big assignment. Harry placed him in charge of the subsidiary Superman Inc., a separate company set up to promote the Superman character and to license the name and likeness to companies seeking to get their products to a growing market of children and teens. The idea was to put the character's name and image on products ranging from toys and cereal boxes to pajamas and lunch pails. Robert Maxwell Joffe—by then going by the less Jewish-sounding name Bob Maxwell—saw Superman Inc. as his route to the more lucrative side of the entertainment business.

SURE ENOUGH, Bob Maxwell thrived in the new role. Working with DC Comics publicity chief Allen Duchovny, he persuaded companies that linking their names to that of Superman would sell their products to a new generation of adolescent consumers. Within a year the Superman name and likeness decorated sweatshirts, baseball caps, greeting cards, dolls, puppets, and pajamas. An 80-foot Superman helium balloon even floated above the crowd at the Macy's Thanksgiving Day Parade. Before long, thousands of kids were spending their nickels and dimes to cover their dues to the Superman fan club (motto: strength—courage—justice). By 1940 the Superman character was showing promise of becoming a multi-million-dollar phenomenon. Fans could read Superman's adventures in both *Action Comics* and the bimonthly *Superman* magazine, which together were selling more than 2.5 million copies per month. The "Superman" newspaper strip—Jerry and Joe's original dream—was appearing in nearly 300 daily and 100 Sunday newspapers. In addition, Max Fleischer Studios would soon release a series of animated cartoons, which opened as part of the Saturday matinee at more than 17,000 theaters nationwide. The Superman empire was taking shape, and Maxwell was in the center of the action.

Jerry and Joe were riding the wave too. They were earning more money and enjoying more fame than they had ever imagined growing up in Glenville. The good pay was particularly useful to Jerry, who had married a girl named Bella from the old neighborhood and wanted to share his good fortune with her. Jerry bought a new house in the nice Jewish neighborhood of Jackson Heights in Queens, another New York City borough, so he could spend more time with an ever-widening circle of bosses, colleagues, and collaborators in the city.

Jerry and Bella also maintained a home in Cleveland, where press coverage of Superman's meteoric rise to fame had made him a local celebrity. Jerry was so well known that neighborhood kids would turn up at his door in search of Superman. Playing along with the game, Jerry would pull his authentic red, blue, and yellow costume out of the closet and whisper that the caped hero would be soaring through the skies of Cleveland later that day. Then he and Bella would pack up for another trip to New York to keep pace with the more experienced, more assertive publishers, editors, and promoters who were driving the business.

Even though the focal point of the Superman enterprise had moved to New York, Joe Shuster stayed put in Cleveland. He used his escalating paycheck to rent a $30-a-month studio and hired a number of art assistants to help keep pace with the mounting workload. This was critical, since poor eyesight was preventing Joe from meeting the demand for more and more comic book and newspaper-strip illustrations on his own. Even in his teens, Joe had squinted through thick lenses at the images on the old, brown butcher paper laid out on his mother's cutting board, but his eyesight had worsened with time.

The added income also allowed Joe to join a health club, where he embarked on a muscle-building regimen that boosted his weight from 112 to 128 pounds, while his hot new platform shoes added an inch to his five-foot-two height. The new look—combined with the status that came from cocreating a popular media figure—seemed to bolster his bravery with women. Joe would often sketch pretty girls at restaurants or outdoor cafés and present the pictures to them as an opening to a conversation, in which he would subtly drop the fact that he had cocreated Superman.

Despite their success, Jerry and Joe had a beef with the world. Back in 1938 they had signed away the Superman copyright to Harry Donenfeld for $130—$10 for each of the 13 pages of *Action Comics* No. 1. True, they were now making well above the standard industry rate and had a ten-year contract that assured them steady work and a good income. But they knew that millions were flowing in from the merchandise sales and media ventures, and most of it was ending up in the pockets of other people. And why should Harry Donenfeld get rich off Superman? He hadn't envisioned the character and spent years perfecting it. As the Cleveland collaborators churned out page after page, week after week, month after month, Donenfeld continued to build the Superman empire, even as he added new superheroes and comic books to his stable. Before long, friends would greet the party-loving publisher in fancy restaurants with the line "Hiya, Superman," at which point he would tear open his shirt and throw out his chest to expose his blue T-shirt with the big red *S* on the front.

The comic book craze that began in the late 1930s would last for decades, as this 1950s photo shows.

CHAPTER 11

"MAYHEM, MURDER, TORTURE, & ABDUCTION"

AS SUPERMAN SOARED TO FAME, he naturally spawned a new line of evil adversaries. His archnemesis, Lex Luthor, premiered in *Action Comics* No. 23. Luthor would live up to his billing as a power-mad, evil scientist of high intelligence and incredible technological prowess. His dedication to killing Superman en route to world dominance never wavered. Superman also spawned dozens of new superheroes. The Man of Steel remained the king of the genre, even as scores of costumed crusaders began soaring through the imaginations of millions of children and adults. Batman and Robin, Hawkman, and the Shadow were soon on newsstands too. At the beginning of 1940 market research studies showed that more than 15 million comic books were sold each month and that five or six kids read each book. One study found that 90 percent of all fourth graders described themselves as regular comic readers.

The growing popularity of comic books gave rise to a chorus of criticism over their perceived effect on young minds. The anti-comic book crusade began on May 8, 1940, with a scathing editorial in the *Chicago Daily News*. Penned by the newspaper's literary editor Sterling North and entitled "A National Disgrace," the editorial assault was based on an examination of 108 comic books. Likening the rise of comic books to a "poisonous mushroom growth," North wrote:

[S]ave for a scattering of more or less innocuous "gag" comics and some reprints of newspaper strips, we found that the bulk of these lurid publications depend for their appeal upon mayhem, murder, torture and abduction— often with a child as the victim. Superman heroics, voluptuous females in scanty attire, blazing machine guns, hooded "justice" and cheap political propaganda were to be found on almost every page.

Warning that tens of millions of copies of these "sex-horror serials are sold every month," North blamed comic books for everything from corrupting young minds to straining young eyes to overstimulating young nervous systems: "Their crude blacks and reds spoil the child's natural sense of color; their hypodermic injection of sex and murder make the child impatient with better, though quieter, stories."

North's answer: Parents should substitute comics with classic children's literature like *Treasure Island*. His diatribe would establish the pillars of an anti-comic book movement that would grow in intensity for decades to come. North was joined by even more vocal critics, including child psychiatrists, psychologists, educators, and political mavericks. In time the anti-comic book crusaders would carry their cause even further. They called upon district attorneys to appoint decency committees that would ban the most offensive publications. The crusaders even incited communities to sponsor comic book burnings outside public schools, where children collected thousands of comic books from their friends and tossed them into roaring bonfires. As the symbol of the genre, Superman was usually the first to burn.

As the anti-comic book crusaders railed against fictional characters, a far more sinister force was stepping out of the shadows in the real world. The Ku Klux Klan was talking of revival and aligning itself with other racist hate groups. The sleeping giant was stirring again.

FOLLOWING THEIR RISE to influence in the 1920s, the national Ku Klux Klan leadership had found themselves steeped in controversy with the federal government breathing down their necks. So the secret order of hooded vigilantes employed the approach it always turned to in times of trouble: It played possum. In the 1930s the national organization dissolved its charter, shut down the Imperial Palace, and told the world it was out of business. Then KKK leaders hunkered down to operate in the shadows and keep the flame of hate and bigotry alive in the United States.

While many Ku Klux Klan chapters did shut down, others continued operating as independent local groups still dedicated to white supremacy, Christian dominance, and rigid morality. While many continued to use the KKK name, language, and garb proudly, others adopted new names to obscure their identities. As the White Cross Clan pressed its racist agenda in Oakland, California, other Klan front groups attacked minorities and preached hate in other cities. By maintaining only loose ties with national KKK leaders, these local groups avoided possible prosecution in federal court as well as the requirement to pay federal taxes. Like-minded local politicians often protected the newly named chapters. Even as the national press wrote the KKK's obituary, local newspapers were writing about radical racist groups operating in their midst.

Then, in the summer of 1940, a bizarre and frightening development took place. As Adolf Hitler's Nazi regime flexed its muscles far away in Europe, resurgent Ku Klux Klan factions began flirting with a new breed of Nazi hate groups in the United States. The Klan was cozying up to the German American Bund, an association led by Nazi sympathizers who praised Hitler, preached fascism, wore Nazi uniforms, and snapped off stiff-armed salutes to flags decorated with a swastika. The powerful and resilient New Jersey Klan led the negotiations with the Bund and arranged a joint rally at a Bund training camp outside Andover, New Jersey.

On August 14, 1940, more than a thousand robed and hooded Klansmen and several hundred gray-shirted Bundsmen assembled on the grounds of Camp Nordland for a day of anti-Semitic speeches and Negro bashing. As the Bundesführer moved to center stage and proclaimed, "The principles of the Bund and the principles of the Klan are the same," the KKK Grand Giant from New Jersey stepped forward and clasped the Bundsman's hand in a show of unity. After the speeches a Klan wedding was held beneath a fiery cross, as if to symbolize a new union between the international and American forms of fascism. As the event reached a crescendo, hundreds of incensed citizens from nearby Andover decided they had had enough of the Nazis and the Klan in their own backyards. The mob gathered at the camp gate and screamed chants like "Burn Hitler on your cross." The forces of hate were threatening to get out of control.

Boy! It's SUPER

Kellogg's

Kellogg's of Battle Creek, Michigan, was the number one name in breakfast cereal and a major sponsor of *The Adventures of Superman.*

CHAPTER 12

ON THE AIR

WITH THE SUPERMAN JUGGERNAUT seemingly moving faster than a speeding bullet, Bob Maxwell turned his attention to an even more alluring prospect: *The Adventures of Superman* on the air. Convinced that a radio program aimed at kids would lift the entire enterprise to new heights, Maxwell and DC Comics press agent Allen Duchovny produced four sample audition discs and began pitching them to potential sponsors and lining up radio stations to carry the show. Early in 1940, Superman made his radio debut in ten selected cities with these words:

**Faster than an airplane.
More powerful than a locomotive.
Impervious to bullets.
Up in the sky—look.
It's a giant bird! It's a plane!
It's Superman.**

And now, Superman—a being no larger than an ordinary man but possessed of powers and abilities never before realized on Earth: able to leap into the air an eighth of a mile at a single bound, hurtle a 20-story building with ease, race a high-powered bullet to its target, lift tremendous weights and rend solid steel in his bare hands as though it were paper. Superman—a strange visitor from a distant planet: champion of the oppressed, physical marvel extraordinary, who has sworn to devote his existence on Earth to helping those in need.

As stations signed on, Bob Maxwell took the helm as producer. He proved to be a hard-driving taskmaster who settled for nothing less than highly entertaining shows with equally high ratings. He knew what he wanted: more excitement! He prodded the writers to produce scripts filled with action and adventure. More tension! He demanded rewrite after rewrite until he felt the script had the right punch. More drama! He made sure the actors, announcers, and sound-effect artists had the chops to turn in top-notch performances. It all added up to more listeners.

As a former pulp writer himself, Maxwell knew he had to make sure that the writers wove liberal doses of good old-fashioned "blood and thunder" into each story arc. At the same time he walked a delicate line as he balanced Superman's thirst for action with his good intentions. Maxwell knew that the show's young listeners—and their parents— prized the wholesome qualities of honesty and fair play. So Superman—by now referred to as the Big Blue Boy Scout by other, edgier comic book superheroes—remained squeaky-clean on the radio.

Jerry Siegel made occasional trips from his New York home in Jackson Heights to the radio studio to watch the production, and he even contributed a couple of scripts that made it on air. He enjoyed being around the fast-paced radio team but knew his place was that of a respected visitor, not a full-fledged team member. Having watched his role in the Superman empire diminish while revenues climbed, he was growing more and more bitter over his role as a wage earner. But for now Jerry kept his anger to himself, and instead fumed internally about how he and Joe were being treated. Still, the Big Blue money machine continued to churn out the green cash. Convinced that he could protect his and Joe's business interests, Jerry turned down advice from friends to consult a lawyer and bode his time. He could make his demand for a greater cut of the profits in the future.

BEFORE LONG AN ELITE TEAM was producing the radio show with flair and panache at the state-of-the-art studios of the Mutual Broadcasting System in Manhattan. Kellogg's of Battle Creek, Michigan—the biggest name in breakfast cereal—sponsored the program. The commercials trumpeted Kellogg's "Pep, the sunshine cereal" with an overly friendly announcer slowly spelling out the letters *P . . . E . . . P* and adding, "Superman says, 'It's super delicious.'"

The radio show remained true to the comic book formula of an all-American hero championing the rights of the little person, while embellishing the story line for kids who enjoyed hearing their favorite characters on the radio as well as reading panel-by-panel adventures in comic books. The radio scriptwriters gave Clark and Lois's newspaper the name the *Daily Planet* and added the roles of cranky editor Perry White and copyboy Jimmy Olsen. They also came up with the liftoff phrase "Up, up, and away!"

and dreamed up the deadly green kryptonite—the rocklike substance from Superman's home planet that drained his powers and left him defenseless. So, day after day at 5:15 p.m., just before the dinner hour, millions of children—and many of their parents—tuned in to hear Superman take on his evil adversaries, swoosh through the sky, plow through mountains, turn back tidal waves, and save Lois Lane from certain death. Each 15-minute mini-drama ended with a dramatic cliff-hanger, followed by a breathless promo for "the next thrilling episode."

The action in the studio was nearly as dynamic as the stories that went out live over the airwaves. With Duchovny directing, the cast crammed their rehearsal time into one hour before the live, on-air performance. Against the backdrop of a large painting of Superman on the studio wall, actors rehearsed their lines, writers tweaked the dialogue, and the three-man sound-effects team tested audio embellishments ranging from bombs exploding to shots firing to crickets chirping. As the studio clock reached the appointed time, announcer Jackson Beck opened the story, and the drama began. The actors read their scripts at a five-foot-tall stand with a microphone that had the network name, MUTUAL, arched above the mouthpiece. Actor Bud Collyer, playing the roles of Clark Kent and Superman, dropped his voice an octave with the words, "This looks like a job for . . . [dramatic pause] Superman!" Actress Joan Alexander captured the spunk of the gutsy Lois Lane, who gushed over the dreamy Superman.

The sound crew used special equipment—or sometimes household items—to create sound effects, such as firing a blank gun to replicate a gunshot or plunging a knife into a melon to replicate a stabbing. The control room also employed a wide range of recorded sound effects, from cheering crowds to shattering glass to racing cars. (The sound of Superman in flight was a mixture of a wind tunnel and an artillery shell.) The Hammond organist enlivened the show with the rousing "March of Superman" and marked tense moments with eerie dramatic tones. And so, day after day, week after week, in episode after episode, Superman battled gangsters, evil scientists, foreign agents, bank robbers, smuggling rings, and corrupt politicians.

The radio show was no more immune to criticism than the comic books were. Some critics claimed that Superman reflected the concept of *der Übermensch*, a German term that could be translated into "the Superman." The term was coined by 19th-century German philosopher Friedrich Nietzsche, who argued that certain people could transcend the influences of religion, culture, and conformity to become enlightened supermen. According to Nietzsche, the person could reach this pinnacle by rising above the pestering of the masses, who buzz like "flies in the marketplace." After Nietzsche's death, the German Nazis twisted his words to mean that their ideal of the blond, blue-eyed German (what they called Aryan) could rise above all "inferiors" to create a dominant race of supermen.

The criticism that Superman manifested a Nazi concept showed a complete lack of understanding of the character. While striving to create a popular superhero who would attract a mass audience, Jerry and Joe had forged Superman to embody the best parts of the American way of life and to raise awareness of "un-American" attitudes. The notion of un-American behavior applied not only to gangsters who broke the law, crooked politicians who violated the public trust, and wealthy industrialists who exploited workers, but also to foreign powers that threatened democracy. So Superman's creators—too busy to be sidetracked by the critics—aimed their superhero at the looming Nazi threat in Europe.

On the cover of *Superman* magazine Lois Lane stands with a Navy sailor, Army soldier, and U.S. Marine. It was part of a carefully planned campaign to support the war effort.

CHAPTER 13

THE SECRET WEAPON

THE CREATORS of the Superman character had been firing their initial salvos at the then undeclared enemy even before the United States entered the war. At first the creators kept their attacks subtle—by comic book standards. Superman writers never mentioned German chancellor Adolf Hitler, Japanese emperor Hirohito, and Italian dictator Benito Mussolini by name, even though it was clear that the jabs and barbs were aimed at these Axis leaders, as well as their ruthless lieutenants, devious spies, and formidable combat troops. Furthermore, Superman's team sought to hammer home to their readers that the foreign dictators followed a philosophy of racial and religious superiority and that their quest for world domination included plans to conquer America.

At about that time, nationally circulated *Look* magazine commissioned Siegel and Shuster to create a strip entitled "How Superman Would End the War." For that special assignment, the collaborators took off their gloves and actually named Hitler as the target. So in the pages of *Look* the caped crusader grabbed the Führer by the scruff of the neck and growled,

"I'd like to land a strictly non-Aryan sock on your jaw." Instead of taking justice into his own hands, however, Superman delivers Hitler to a tribunal of world leaders to face justice. In another direct challenge in a Superman newspaper strip the caped crusader demolishes part of the German Westwall with France.

That's when Superman's fictionalized triumphs over the Nazis came to the attention of the German ministerial bureau that tracked foreign press commentary. The German propagandists did not respond well to the Superman stories, and the U.S. press covered their response. U.S. newspaper reports that infamous Nazi propaganda minister Joseph Goebbels exploded in a meeting over the Superman anti-Nazi crusades were almost certainly exaggerated if not outright false. But it is true that *Das Schwarze Korps,* the weekly newspaper of the infamous Nazi Secret Service, denounced Superman. In April 1940 the paper ran the proclamation, "Superman *ist ein Jude!*" ("Superman is a Jew!") The sarcastic, mocking piece referred to Superman's primary creator as Jerry "Israel" Siegel and accused him of sowing "hate, suspicion, evil, laziness, and criminality in young hearts":

Jerry Siegel, an intellectually and physically circumcised chap who has his headquarters in New York, is the inventor of a colorful figure with an impressive appearance, a powerful body, and a red swim suit who enjoys the ability to fly through the ether.

The inventive Israelite named this pleasant guy with an overdeveloped body and underdeveloped mind "Superman." He advertised widely Superman's sense of

justice, well-suited for imitation by the American youth.
As you can see, there is nothing the Sadducees [an
ancient Jewish sect] won't do for money! Jerry Siegellack
stinks. Woe to the American youth who must live in such a
poisonous environment and don't even notice the poison
they are swallowing daily.

Superman *did* reflect the culture of his Jewish creators. The Jewish-American story was baked into the personality of his character and his exploits. Superman also seemed to reflect the more modern—and frightening—Jewish realities of the time. The story of baby Superman's journey from Krypton seemed to foreshadow the saga of the Kindertransports—the emergency evacuations of hundreds of Jewish children, without their parents, from Nazi Germany to safety in Great Britain prior to the war.

FOLLOWING THE JAPANESE ATTACK on Pearl Harbor and the U.S. entrance into the war against the Axis alliance, Americans moved to a total war footing. Troops shipped off for combat; industry shifted to the production of planes, ships, and munitions; and newspapers covered all aspects of the raging conflict. Thousands of women began trading their housedresses and aprons for work shirts and khaki slacks to train as welders, riveters, mechanics, and machinists. Their mission was to help transform the nation's aircraft plants, shipyards, and factories into an industrial war machine.

Leading columnists issued clarion calls for the defense of democracy and braced their readers for a long, bloody struggle to come. The U.S. War

Department set up the Office of Censorship to review, amend, or stop all media reports that could disclose sensitive information on war strategy, troop locations, or weapons development. It was a new day in America. And comic book publishers sent a new line of superpatriotic characters like Captain America and the Star-Spangled Kid into action.

Like most Americans, the Superman creative team foresaw the long road ahead and knew that victory hinged on the effectiveness of the nation's leadership and the bravery and blood of its fighting men. The creators wanted to use Superman to support the war effort, but there was a problem, which *Time* dubbed "Superman's Dilemma." Given the character's power to soar to the sky, to change the course of mighty rivers, to turn back tidal waves, and to survive massive explosions without a scratch, it only stood to reason that he could single-handedly defeat the enemy in short order. More specifically, Superman ought to be able to drop thousand-pound bombs from the sky on German troops, flick Japanese Zeros out of the air, and drag battleships to the bottom of the ocean.

In the end the editors decided against publishing what would certainly be several years of highly implausible Superman combat adventures. Instead Superman would be stationed at home in Metropolis and would make only periodic visits to the front lines to support the troops or to handle delicate, secret missions for the top brass. In Metropolis he would serve as a role model for life on the home front, and his encounters with villains like Lex Luthor, the Prankster, the Toyman, and the Insect Master would provide readers with an escape from the weighty issues of the war.

Once the home-front strategy was set, the writers needed a plot device to explain why the Man of Steel was not joining the Army, Navy, or Marines and going off to war with the rest of the troops. The solution appeared in the "Superman" newspaper strips that ran from February 15 to February 19, 1942. The story begins with Clark Kent arriving at his recruitment center to sign up for duty. The bumbling reporter is so excited about joining the armed forces that he inadvertently botches his eye exam. The reason: His x-ray vision kicks in, and he accidently reads the eye chart in an adjacent room. The doctors declare him 4-F (undraftable) and send him packing. As a result, in the pages of *Superman* comics, Kent does not don a military uniform for the duration, and Superman is free to influence the war as an outsider.

The homebound Superman encourages Americans to buy war bonds, to ration scarce supplies, and to donate to organizations like the Red Cross and the United Services Organization (USO). In his adventures, Superman travels outside Metropolis to military training centers to lift the spirits of the troops and to prepare them for the action ahead. In one comic book adventure he travels to a fictional U.S. military training center, where he takes part in a mock war game by taking the side of the blue army in a simulated battle with the red army. Superman ferries blue troops across rivers, bombs red airfields with sandbags, locates red snipers with his x-ray vision, and finally tunnels through a mountain to lead blue troops into the red camp. Facing defeat, the red general implores his men to fight on. "What if they were Japs or Nazis?" he asks. "Would you let down the folks who are counting on you to save your country and the world?" At this point the red army summons the strength to repel the blues and win the game. Superman, happily experiencing a rare defeat, concludes that American soldiers are the real superheroes and congratulates the men for being "Super-Soldiers."

Still, from 1941 to 1945 there were stories of Superman's periodic trips to the front lines. Siegel clearly designed one newspaper strip to draw the attention of American children to the evil of the enemy. In this strip, Hitler, Mussolini, and Tojo (Japan's prime minister) kidnap Santa Claus as part of their plan for world domination. Superman is forced to rescue Old Saint Nick and save Christmas.

In addition to these occasional war stories, a number of powerful *Superman* magazine covers trumpeted the war effort, even though there were usually no corresponding stories inside to back up the symbolic cover art: Superman, seen through the periscope of a German U-boat, swimming furiously toward the submarine in the wake of the Allied ship that the sub just sank; Superman holding an eagle on his arm, standing proudly in front of the Stars and Stripes; Superman delivering supplies to an American machine-gun squad fighting in the jungles; Lois Lane, with an Army soldier, a Navy sailor, and a Marine, telling them with a wink, "You're my Supermen."

Through the war years the radio version of Superman, like his counterpart in print, did his part to turn back the Axis powers. In a bid to create the ultimate German villain, the scriptwriters dreamed up Nazi scientist der Teufel (the name means "the Devil" in German). Der Teufel swallows a dose of radioactive kryptonite to turn himself into Atom Man, whose whole existence is dedicated to killing Superman. Der Teufel's plot fails.

In 1943, toward the end of the war, Jerry Siegel's draft number came up, and he took his place with the American troops. As he was a minor celebrity, his send-off was held at a Freedom Day celebration on the Fourth of July in Cleveland, and his duty entailed serving on the staff of the military newspaper *Stars and Stripes*. As he penned illustrations for the military newspaper and got a taste of army discipline by peeling potatoes, Siegel had plenty of time to think about what might happen to his Superman role while he was away—and while Donenfeld and Liebowitz were banking the revenues generated by the character that Siegel and Shuster had created. For his par, Joe Shuster was exempt from service due to his failing eyesight; he had flunked an eye test like the one Clark Kent failed in the comics.

But perhaps Superman's most important war contribution was his direct connection to the troops. The scene of a soldier or sailor passing time with a comic book in hand was common overseas, and Superman was the superhero of choice for most of the servicemen and women. In fact, one of four magazines shipped to troops overseas was a comic book, and 35,000 copies of *Superman* alone went abroad each month. The U.S. War Department and USO made sure that copies of *Superman* magazine were distributed to soldiers, sailors, and marines throughout the war. Military leaders hoped to provide a little entertainment and escape until the troops could come back home for good. As *Time* reported, "Superman got a high priority rating last week: the Navy Department ruled that Superman comic books should be included among essential supplies destined for the marine garrison at Midway Islands. For the tough Marines, as for all U.S. Armed Forces, the Man of Steel is still super-favorite reading."

Stetson Kennedy tracked white supremacist groups by collecting their hate sheets and newsletters. In full Klan regalia, he displays white-power literature at a 1947 press conference.

CHAPTER 14

FIGHTING HATE AT HOME

KEPT OUT OF THE SERVICE by a bad back, Stetson Kennedy
spent the war years tracking the forces of organized hate back in the
United States. "I resolved to fight fascists in my own backyard," he
recalled later. Kennedy figured that battling the Klan and homegrown
Nazi organizations was a worthy contribution to the cause of democracy, particularly since so many of his friends had shipped off for duty
abroad. Kennedy had moved on from his work as a folklorist to become
a writer and activist with a clear bead on organized hate in the United
States. He moved his base of operation from South Florida to Atlanta,
the spiritual home of the modern KKK and a perceived safe haven for
other extremist groups. It was a perfect perch for watching his adversaries and reporting on their activities.

Kennedy penned dozens of exposés for newspapers ranging from the
left-leaning *PM* to the African-American *Pittsburgh Courier.* Under his
byline flowed account after account of Ku Klux Klan violence, political
influence, and rituals, as well as predictions of an imminent KKK revival.

Kennedy also went to work for a number of organizations that sought to expose and undercut organized hate groups like the Klan and the Nazis. By the spring of 1944 he was going after his enemies with all the confidence and zeal of a real-life Superman, even adopting a secret identity to penetrate their ranks.

One of Kennedy's most important clients was the Atlanta branch of the Anti-Defamation League (ADL) of B'nai B'rith, an organization dedicated to preventing the defamation of the Jewish people and protecting the rights of all. Kennedy's friends at the ADL set him up with false identification as an itinerant encyclopedia salesman named John S. Perkins. As Perkins, Kennedy subscribed to dozens of hate sheets published by organizations such as the American Gentile Army, the White Front, the Christian Front, and the Union of Christian Crusaders. He continued to cozy up to the Klan.

Kennedy also worked for an organization called the Non-Sectarian Anti-Nazi League, usually referred to simply as the Anti-Nazi League (ANL). Formed by Jewish intellectuals and businessmen before the war to raise awareness of the German threat, the ANL was now focusing on homegrown hate groups. And it was hiring spies to infiltrate them.

IN THOSE DAYS one of Kennedy's biggest challenges was remembering who he was supposed to be at any given moment. While playing the role of hatemonger John Perkins, it could have been fatal to slip up and reveal his true identity as the writer, activist, union organizer, and Klan buster Stetson Kennedy. "I had to remember to keep in mind where I was and who I was talking to," he would recall later. "This meant a dual life, somewhat precarious."

There were many other important voices rising up against the Klan, and many of those voices emanated from the KKK stronghold of Atlanta. Taking on the KKK with the power of his pen, Ralph McGill, the crusading editor of the *Atlanta Journal-Constitution,* often wrote to his readers in the tone of a parent assuring his children that their fears and prejudices were unwarranted:

There are not many Catholics in Georgia which is a pity in a way because they are almost invariably good Christians, good citizens and worthwhile members of the community, something which has not been possible to say because of all the members of the Ku Klux Klan klaverns in the state ... There are not many Jews in Georgia either but they, too, are good citizens. Their contribution is one of hard work and decency. There is no reason to have an organization formed to promote hate and antagonism to Catholics, Jews, foreign-born citizens or any minority groups ... If you could get through all the mumbo jumbo business of the kleagels, Cyclops, nighthawks and all the claptrap, you would still find it to be silly, unchristian and dangerous to the peace and dignity of the people.

Assistant Attorney General Daniel Duke of Georgia also took on the Ku Klux Klan in Atlanta. The hard-charging prosecutor had sent a number of Klansmen to prison for violent attacks against blacks and accused moral backsliders in the 1930s and early 1940s, and he was determined to see the guilty parties serve out their sentences. Late in 1941 Georgia governor Eugene Talmadge suggested granting clemency to the convicted floggers. This triggered a showdown between the fiery prosecutor and the race-baiting governor, who had long pandered for votes from KKK leaders and their followers. At a public hearing on the proposed pardons, Duke held up two leather whips with KKK etched into the handles and waved them in Talmadge's face while making the point that the Klan's weapon of choice could stop a bull elephant. Unmoved by the argument, Talmadge stated that he was familiar with such whips because he had once used one on a black man. Talmadge would go on to curry votes from the Klan and Duke would stand against them for years to come.

PART FOUR

COLLISION

After the war, the world seemed like a different place. The horrors of the Holocaust were fresh in the public mind. German war criminals were on trial in Nuremberg, Germany. With the goal of preventing another global conflagration, world leaders were forming the United Nations in New York City. Soldiers were mustering out of the military, buying homes, and starting families. The first automatic clothes dryers were on sale at Sears, Superman was looking for a new villain, and the Ku Klux Klan was planning a revival. Over a frenetic one-year period, the Man of Steel and the men of hate would pursue their separate paths—and then collide.

Bud Collyer was the voice of both Clark Kent and Superman on the long-running *The Adventures of Superman* radio show. He is shown here enjoying an issue of *Superman* magazine.

CHAPTER 15

OPERATION INTOLERANCE

AS WORLD WAR II CAME TO AN END, the radio producers of *The Adventures of Superman* were looking for a new villain. The show was drawing more than four million listeners to the nearly 200 Mutual stations nationwide and garnering solid ratings. But even a successful kids' radio program had to change with the times. The old enemies—Nazi agents, German scientists, foreign dictators, and Japanese traitors—were no longer relevant. Even the standard villains of mobsters, monsters, mad scientists, criminal masterminds, and supernatural forces seemed exhausted. On top of that, the parent-teacher organizations and child psychologists were still at it. They claimed that kids' radio held out violence as the answer to every conceivable problem for a generation of over-stimulated youth. Seeking a new direction, the producers of *The Adventures of Superman* asked a tough question: What next?

Shortly after the end of the war, that question was bandied about the luxurious Park Avenue offices of Kenyon and Eckhardt, the advertising agency that represented Kellogg's and managed its link to *The Adventures of Superman.* The agency played an active role in the show and provided vital support to the producers, cast, and crew. For example, it employed a crack team of decoders to decipher thousands of letters that Superman fans wrote to their hero in secret code.

Contemplating the future of the program, K&E vice president William B. Lewis asked a fascinating question: What if *The Adventures of Superman* tackled contemporary social issues like racism and anti-Semitism? There had been plenty of stories about racist, hatemongering organizations in the New York press, and the issue wasn't going away anytime soon. So why not take it on? What if they used Superman to teach children the values of tolerance and fair play and the importance of accepting other kids regardless of race, religion, or national origin? What if Superman could teach a generation of children to reject those who preached prejudice and hate? After all, the entire country had banded together to win the war. Now most everyone was banding together to build a peaceful and prosperous future. Those grim photographs and films of mass graves and starving concentration camp prisoners had made an indelible mark on the public mind. Could Superman lead the way? Lewis thought so. "We're not in the business of education," he said. "We're selling corn flakes. But we'd like to do both. We sure would like to do both."

BOB MAXWELL JUMPED at the chance to lead the campaign. He also knew it had a good chance of bombing. The most obvious risk was that the shows would come across as preachy or dull to a mass audience of kids raised on the fantasy, thrills, and spills of adventure radio. If bored or confused listeners tuned out, the ratings would plummet, the sponsor would howl, and the network honchos would demand a return to the standard fare of blood and thunder. "You'll lose your audience," one skeptical associate reportedly told Maxwell at the outset of the project. "Children want straight, unadulterated entertainment." Other kids' radio shows had produced educational programs with disappointing results. Those programs had traded their sizzle for serious messages and, after losing large segments of the audience, had quickly returned to the tried-and-true formula of murder, mystery, and mayhem.

Despite the pitfalls, Maxwell believed that the potential payoff outweighed the risk. By producing outstanding shows with the theme of tolerance, *The Adventures of Superman* could set a new standard for educational programming for the entire broadcast industry. In addition a successful campaign would spur a torrent of positive publicity. The broadcast trade publications would praise the producers for their vision and follow-through, and the mainstream press would herald Kellogg's as an enlightened corporate sponsor. The breakthrough shows might even make allies of the growing coalition of parents, teachers, and psychologists railing against the violence in kids' radio.

Then there was Maxwell's other reason for embracing the effort. His current observance of Jewish tradition may have consisted of downing the occasional lox and bagel at the corner deli and gathering with family on holidays, but he still wanted to do his part. After all, the world knew that six million Jews had died in the Nazi death camps. Didn't everyone have a duty to make sure this atrocity never happened again? Maybe he could make a contribution by teaching young Superman fans to reject prejudice and to embrace tolerance. Besides, he had watched his father win awards and accolades for his humanitarian service. He wanted that for his radio show—and himself.

Looking ahead to the Operation Intolerance campaign, Maxwell knew one thing for sure: Entertainment had to trump education. The programs would have to be fast paced and full of adventure. Each episode would have to end with a compelling cliff-hanger to make listeners come back the next day. Superman's adversaries would have to be just as frightening as the criminal masterminds and mad scientists of old. That meant taking on real-world hatemongers like neo-Nazi thugs and hooded Klansmen and not pulling any punches. In preparation for the launch, Maxwell and company reportedly reviewed 25 scripts that failed to hit the mark. "The difficulty was that, while most of the writers were adept at the melodramatic, cliffhanging, hair-breadth escape techniques necessary for a show like Superman, few knew how to weave the social point of view artfully into the story," the newspaper *PM* reported.

The show's producers finally found the answer in Ben Peter Freeman, a former *New York Times* reporter who was making a name for himself as a first-rate freelancer around town. Freeman had proved himself to *The Adventures of Superman* over the previous year, as he had tapped his potent imagination to pen a number of popular episodes including "The Scarlet Widow," which featured one of the few female master criminals to clash with the Man of Steel. Beyond his obvious creative flair, Freeman's background as a journalist was also helpful to Operation Intolerance, since the final scripts would have to accurately reflect the reality of organized hate in America.

Even with a solid wordsmith on board, there were other potential pitfalls. What if a 12-year-old white boy from the Midwest tuned in to an episode just long enough to hear a bigoted character taunt a Negro girl? Might the impressionable listener imitate the racist behavior? What if a teenager tuned in to a scene in which a youth gang desecrated a synagogue? Could that young listener get the mistaken notion that such behavior was OK or, worse, that Superman endorsed it? The other risk was that programs based on real-life hate groups could scare kids half to death. What if a little girl ran to her parents and asked, "Will those men in hoods and robes tar and feather our family too?"

Maxwell knew that the job required a deep understanding of children and education. He believed in fully researching potential show themes and went all out on this campaign. He first turned to education consultant Josette Frank, a researcher for the Child Study Association of America (CSAA). The bookish and well-spoken Miss Frank had lobbied Maxwell to be part of his effort of "shaping a new form of radio entertainment for children." Miss Frank had challenged him to go beyond portraying "heroes for heroism's sake," adding that "kids are invested in the future and their part in it." She jokingly assured Maxwell, "I am seething with ideas for you to throw out." She believed that the radio producers could infuse educational messages with enough excitement to make kids "drop their baseball bats and rush to their dials." As the work on the script continued, Miss Frank began soliciting advice from organizations ranging from the Big Brothers of America to the National Conference of Christian and Jews. She ran sample scripts by the leaders of those organizations and channeled the feedback to the writers and producers. Knowing that strong scripts and careful research were essential, she told Maxwell, "Only the children can give it success!"

Miss Frank was well known to the Superman team. In the late 1930s, while consulting with DC Comics on complaints of violent and sexually explicit content, she proved to be an expert the editors could work with.

She was far more open-minded than the hard-core critics who blamed comics for everything from high dropout rates to teenage sex. In contrast, Miss Frank pointed out that millions of kids actually *chose* to read comic books and learned valuable lessons from the plot twists and usual triumph of good over evil. Still, Miss Frank was no pushover. In a letter to the publisher of *Wonder Woman,* she once wrote, "This feature does lay you open to considerable criticism . . . partly on the basis of the woman's costume (or lack of it), and partly on the basis of sadistic bits showing women chained, tortured, etc." Despite her concerns, Miss Frank probably saw value in Wonder Woman's decidedly feminine superpowers—she could deflect bullets with her bracelets—as well as her sensible advice to abused women: "Get strong! Earn your own living—Remember, the better you can fight, the less you'll have to!"

Miss Frank even called a luncheon meeting at the American Museum of Natural History with famed cultural anthropologist Margaret Mead, who advised Maxwell to step carefully with—as the agenda put it—"stories dramatizing, realistically or by allegory, the fight against threats to democracy—fascism, intolerance, mob run, vigilante movements." Mead advised that tense drama on racial or religious conflict might be "inappropriate to the building up of serene attitudes." Maxwell responded, "What makes you think there is any serenity in children's programming?"

With serenity put in its proper place, the first scripts came together, and Operation Intolerance got the final go-ahead. The first on-air reference to the program came that winter, in 1946. On February 5 announcer Jackson Beck intoned a new opening: "Yes, it's Superman. Strange visitor from another planet, who came to earth with powers and abilities far beyond those of mortal men. Superman, defender of law and order, champion of equal rights, valiant, courageous fighter against the forces of hate and prejudice!"

On April 16, 1946, millions of children tuned in at the appointed hour to begin an exciting new series. This time Superman would not be battling mad scientists, atomic weapons, and supernatural menaces; he would not be turning back tidal waves and breaking up smuggling rings. This time America's favorite superhero would be declaring war on religious bigots and racist extremists. The first installment was titled "The Hate Mongers Organization." The story went like this:

ON THE STREETS of Metropolis at midnight, two shadowy figures approach Hoffman's Drug Store on Morton Street. As one of the thugs heaves a rock through the display window, the other douses the building with gasoline. The young hoodlums then light a fire that quickly destroys the drugstore and engulfs the entire city block.

It turns out the arsonists are foot soldiers of the Guardians of America, a secretive group of Nazi-like terrorists run by a racist and religious bigot who goes by the name Frank Hill. Hill and his gang of teenage thugs are out to stop the Metropolis Interfaith Council from building a community clubhouse and gymnasium "for the use of all boys and girls in the neighborhood, regardless of race, creed or color . . . where children of every race, ethnic background and spiritual belief can play and learn that all people are alike." Inspired by Hill's hateful rhetoric, his band of misguided "juvenile delinquents" steps up its violent attacks against supporters of the proposed community center. The Guardians invade a Jewish temple and stab a rabbi. They beat up a Catholic boy who witnessed an arson.

As the tension mounts, Clark Kent explains the grim reality to cub reporter Jimmy Olsen—and to the millions of impressionable young listeners glued to their radios. "It isn't just the Catholics, or the Jews, or the Protestants they're after," the mild-mannered reporter explains. "Their game is to stir up hatred among all of us—to get the Catholic to hate the Jew and the Jew to hate the Protestant, and the Protestant to hate the Catholic. It's a dirty, vicious circle, and like Hitler and his Nazi killers, they plan to step in and pick up the marbles while we're busy hating one another and cutting each other's throats. It's an old trick but for some reason a lot of us still fall for it."

Jimmy Olsen has gone undercover to infiltrate the Guardians. He gains the trust of the gang and arranges a rare meeting with Frank Hill. Jimmy meets Hill in the group's penthouse headquarters and pretends to embrace the Guardians' mission. Then Jimmy is stunned to learn that a respected community leader—a purported backer of the unity house project—is really a secret supporter of the Guardians. The turncoat knows of Jimmy's close ties to Clark Kent and exposes him as a mole. His cover blown, Jimmy is bound, gagged, thrown in the back of a car, taken to the Metropolis bridge, and tossed in the river. As Jimmy sinks toward almost certain death, Superman soars to his rescue, plunging into the river and lifting him to safety.

Then the Man of Steel flies to the Guardians' headquarters to round up Hill and his gang. He searches the headquarters and finds documents showing that Frank Hill is actually Franz Hiller, a former Nazi spy with a grand plan to impose a fascist dictatorship on the United States. The young gang members are shocked to learn that Hiller had manipulated them. In the end, the Man of Steel warns the gang members:

Remember this as long as you live: Whenever you meet up with anyone who is trying to cause trouble between people—anyone who tries to tell you that a man can't be a good citizen because of his religious beliefs— you can be sure that the troublemaker is a rotten citizen himself and a rotten human being. Don't ever forget that!

The radio team was elated. The ratings for "The Hate Mongers Organization" pushed *The Adventures of Superman* to the number one children's show on air. The praise from the press just added to the euphoria. The CSAA applauded the "use of children's own favorite medium to . . . combat the spread of race and religious bigotry." Serving dozens of African-American newspapers, the Calvin Newspaper Service applauded "this noble effort to make better citizens of our children and to eradicate from their minds all thoughts of racial and religious intolerance." The National Conference of Christians and Jews encouraged other broadcasters to "follow the lead of Superman."

"The Hate Mongers Organization," however, was just an opening salvo in the show's war on bigotry. In this episode the producers had played it safe by pitting Superman against an adversary like Franz Hiller. Germany's Nazi threat was still fresh in the public mind, and Hiller was not that much different from the Nazi villains Superman had conquered during the war. Now the creative team was preparing to take on a dire and truly American threat to democracy: the Ku Klux Klan. The timing was perfect.

Klansmen initiate new members into the Invisible Empire in a haunting ceremony atop Stone Mountain outside Atlanta.

CHAPTER 16

RETURN TO STONE MOUNTAIN

THE EVENTS OF MAY 9, 1946, in Atlanta were not fantasy. Late that night a 300-foot-tall wooden cross burned on a granite butte near the top of Stone Mountain. The flames cast a glow over more than a thousand men clad in white robes and hoods. Distinguished by his flowing green robe, Ku Klux Klan Grand Dragon Samuel Green presided from a makeshift altar made of flagstones, draped with an American flag, and bedecked with an unsheathed sword, a canteen of water, and a Bible open to Romans 12: The Christian Life. As plumes of flame leaped into the night and a half moon rose in the distant sky, the Grand Dragon delivered a blistering call to arms in defense of white rule. Bringing his racist rant to a crescendo, he cast his gaze on several dozen men kneeling before him in plain clothes. After leading the new recruits in the sacred oath of initiation, he declared them knights of the Ku Klux Klan. He also warned that betrayal of the organization's secrets would result in the ultimate punishment: death at the hands of a brother. As the ceremony ended Green cried, "We are revived!"

Grand Dragon Green was elated with the Stone Mountain coming-out party. More than 200 new recruits had been initiated that night, and more than a thousand spectators had trekked up the mountain to witness the event. Major newspapers, national wire services, and a nationally circulated magazine had covered it, and most reporters had used adjectives like "eerie," "mysterious," "awesome," and "haunting" to describe the goings-on. In fact the next issue of *LIFE* magazine featured a four-page photo spread under the headline "Ku Klux Klan Tries a Comeback. It Pledges Initiates in a Mystic Pageant on Georgia's Stone Mountain." Now millions of readers across the country had the message that Green wanted them to have: The KKK was rising again.

Green—a 54-year-old physician with wire-frame spectacles and a small, bushy white moustache—planned to follow the public relations coup with a highly organized national membership drive that would attract legions of new followers to the reviving order. A longtime Klansman and dedicated follower of the late colonel William Simmons, Doc Green planned to apply the historic philosophies, rituals, and methods of the Klan to the emerging social conditions of post-World War II America. Just as Superman's creators kept and built their audience by adjusting their hero as times changed, Green would do the same to attract his army of "100 percent Americans."

In preparation for the revival, Green had done his homework. Traveling the country to test public sentiment, he had found reason to believe that millions of white protestant men from Connecticut to California, from Michigan to Mississippi, would respond to the call. With black military veterans mustering out of the service and seeking equal rights in the country they had fought for, Green wanted to tap in to white fear. To avoid potential entanglements with the federal government, he named his organization the Association of Georgia Klans, and he accepted the role of Grand Dragon of the Georgia Realm (as opposed to Imperial Wizard of the entire empire) for the time being. At the same time, he began strengthening ties to KKK realms in Tennessee, Oregon, California, New Jersey, and many other states. After pulling together Klan groups across the country, he planned to reestablish Atlanta as the imperial capital and to reign over the whole organization. There was evidence the revival was taking hold. In Mississippi, Hodding Carter, crusading editor of the *Delta Democrat-Times*, warned that the Invisible Empire was "sloshing over like an overfull cesspool from its stronghold in Georgia."

What Green didn't fully understand was that his organization had been badly compromised. The Georgia Department of Law had placed undercover agents inside Klavern No. I, and the FBI was watching and listening too. Stetson Kennedy had seen the revival coming and had stepped up his Klan-busting activities. In early 1946 he had scored an application to the Invisible Empire of the Knights of the Ku Klux Klan in Atlanta. It read:

To his majesty the Imperial Wizard: I the undersigned, a native born true citizen of the United States, being a white male gentile person of temperate habits, sound of mind and a believer in the tenets of the Christian religion and white supremacy and the principles of a pure Americanism, do most respectfully apply for membership in the Knights of the Ku Klux Klan, through Klavern No I, Realm of Georgia.

Kennedy (as his alter ego Perkins) got in, purchased a ten-dollar robe and hood, and began ingratiating himself to the hatemongers. He spewed the same kind of racial epithets that dominated their conversations, all the while collecting information to use against them. Continuing to glean information from scores of white-supremacist newsletters, he stepped up his efforts to spread the word by working his intelligence into his articles and leaking information to friendly journalists.

Also in 1946, Kennedy published his most important book, *Southern Exposure*. In it he revealed the workings of organized hate groups and laid out what he saw as the underlying causes of racism in the Deep South. Described by journalists of his day as mild mannered and slight of build, with thinning blond hair, Kennedy made sure his *Southern Exposure* book tour would be a low-key affair. In an attempt to stay hidden from his contacts within the hate groups, he allowed no picture of himself on the book jacket and refused to let newspapers photograph him. As it turned out, one journalist almost blew Kennedy's cover by describing him as having the face of a poet, which would have the hatemongers asking who that might be.

The *St. Petersburg Times* review of *Southern Exposure* didn't need a photo. It featured a drawing of a robed and hooded man being speared by a fountain pen. This captured Kennedy's chosen mode of combat: attack by press release. Kennedy reveled in the role of muckraking journalist, issuing blaring headlines and breathless prose and dreaming up sensational publicity stunts to warn of the KKK threat and the evils of racism. Through the years his methods would become more extreme and controversial, and his critics would accuse him of sensationalism, grandstanding, and shameless self-promotion.

DESPITE KENNEDY'S best efforts to infiltrate, however, the author and activist was only going to get so far inside the Klan. He needed help. By the spring of 1946, Kennedy had the help he needed to forge a direct pipeline into the deepest secrets of the Atlanta Klan. As part of his services to the ANL and ADL, Kennedy worked as the handler for a top-secret, deeply embedded mole who was operating under the alias John Brown. "This worker is joining the Klan for me," Kennedy wrote in one memo to his employers in early 1946. "I am certain that he can be relied on."

Brown was a former Klansman who had come to see the true nature of the hooded order and had committed himself to lifting the cover off its violent actions and conspiracies. He still had the complete trust of the KKK leadership, and he used it to burrow deep into the inner sanctum of the infamous Nathan Bedford Forrest Klavern No. 1, which met every Monday night at a cavernous union hall at 198½ Whitehall Street. Brown's reports detailed KKK plans for the major revival that took place a year later on Stone Mountain, attacks on Negroes moving into white neighborhoods, and the involvement of Atlanta police officers in KKK violence. By Brown's own count, 83 of the 200 men in Klavern No. 1 were Atlanta police officers, many of whom regularly directed traffic and provided security at cross burnings.

Brown's reports were chilling. In a dispatch dated April 29, 1946, he reported that Grand Dragon Samuel Green was advised to "write a letter of appreciation to a policeman named 'Itchy Trigger Finger' Nash . . . in connection with the slaying of a Negro on Decatur Street last week. This makes the thirteenth Negro he has killed in his line of duty. It seems that Dr. Green would like to decorate these policemen who kill Negros with the Klan."

Brown even infiltrated the paramilitary flog squad that carried out midnight whippings, beatings, and murders of selected targets. Or, as handler Kennedy reported to the ANL on May 6, 1946, "our informant is now a member of the Klan's inner circle, the Klavalier Klub." Kennedy went on to note, "[O]ur informant has learned that Green is an honorary member and bears card No. 000 . . . Obviously the Klavalier Klub is the Storm Trooper arm of the Klan and there is some effort to divorce the regular Klan officials from responsibility of its actions." Brown even got inside a secret subunit of the Klavalier Klub that called itself the Ass-Tearers and printed on its calling card the image of a corkscrew—its implement of choice for torturing and disemboweling its victims.

The infiltrators' reports painted a haunting picture of KKK conspiracies and violence, as well as the paranoid mentality that pervaded the Klavern. The reports detail hit lists targeting anti-Klan journalists and even plots to steal weapons caches from government stockpiles to use in an all-out onslaught against African Americans. Even the mundane matters described in the reports are eye-opening, from membership drives and publicity campaigns to ham dinners put on by the ladies' auxiliary to raise money for their husbands' work.

The moles centered much of their attention on Grand Dragon Green and his top henchmen of the Associated Klans of Georgia. As overseer of Klavern No. 1, Green had virtually invited the scrutiny of investigators with his militant call for white protestant men across the country to rise up and take the nation back from the Negroes, Jews, Catholics, and liberals. While Green insisted the Klan was breaking no laws, the undercover operatives knew that beyond the violent raids that the KKK was carrying out, Green and company were also acting as the central players in a resurgent national KKK movement, coordinating with Klaverns in other states and even supplying them with membership forms and propaganda pamphlets printed in Atlanta. If the Klan busters could prove that the Atlanta Klavern was acting as the center of a national program, they could push Georgia to revoke the organization's state charter, thus leaving Green and company open to federal income tax debt and possible prosecution in federal court. And to top it all off, a kids' radio show was about to lift the mask off the KKK for a generation of children.

When the Superman team approached leaders of the Anti-Defamation League for input about the radio programs, they must have felt as if they had hit the mother lode: access to secret information coming straight from the inner sanctum of the most dangerous Klan in the country. The precise nature of the communication among the New York producers, the ADL staff, and the infiltrators remains murky to this day. It appears that no written correspondence took place, and personal accounts vary.

Stetson Kennedy insists that he gave the producers the idea for the anti-Klan broadcasts after watching kids at play; apparently he figured that a kids' radio drama starring the "fabulous jet propelled character" could show a generation of youth the perils of prejudice. "Armed with complete information about the Klan's set up, rituals and roles played by Cyclopes, Terrors, Ghouls and Titans, they wrote a series of programmes," Kennedy later recalled. This is not the only claim of Kennedy's that doesn't match other accounts, but, whatever the exact communication was, it is clear that information did flow from Atlanta through the ADL to the producers of Superman. Bob Maxwell and his team could proceed, knowing they had solid information to base their show on.

The fiery cross became the flaming symbol of the KKK, as evidenced by this cross burning outside Midvale, New Jersey, in 1940.

CHAPTER 17

"CLAN OF THE FIERY CROSS"

AS THE KLAN GRABBED for more power and the infiltrators moved to stop them, *The Adventures of Superman* radio team focused on the task at hand. The goal was to create a highly engaging, action-packed, 16-part series dramatizing the realities of the Ku Klux Klan to a generation of young radio listeners.

The creative team approached the series with care to avoid a direct conflict with the real Klan. Aware that the reviving order was centered in Atlanta, the radio team knew that any organized criticism would likely come from that city. In writing the script, the name Ku Klux Klan would be replaced with a made-up name to avoid any potential entanglement with an organization that operated under a legal charter in the state of Georgia and in other states. The central character in the show—and the prime target of the hatemongers—would not be African American. This would counter the stereotypical belief that the Klan targeted only blacks. In this series the fictional hate peddlers would target a Chinese-American boy and his family. The script would not use dialect or accents to distinguish characters by race, religion, or geographic region. This was not about condemning southerners or stereotyping minority groups. This was about teaching tolerance to millions of young listeners—and showing just how destructive prejudice could be. Even Superman's heroics would be scaled back to allow the human characters to play heroes too. This would teach young listeners that ordinary people can stand up to bigotry.

Despite the delicate touch, the script would still have to reflect the Klan's racism, violence, and greed. The story line would have to be action-packed, with plenty of cliff-hangers to keep the audience coming back. The condemnation of bigotry would have to be clear and absolute. There could be no room for misunderstanding. By the summer of 1946 the stage was set, the actors had their roles, and the drama was ready to start. As Grand Dragon Green basked in the glow of his Stone Mountain revival and as Stetson Kennedy and John Brown dug deeper into the ranks of Klavern No. 1, the 16-part "Clan of the Fiery Cross" went live. The first episode aired on June 10, 1946.

THE STORY BEGINS with Jimmy Olsen, who is managing the baseball team sponsored by Unity House—a recreational center for kids of diverse races, religions, and ethnic backgrounds. The Unity House team has won a spot in the city playoffs on the strength of star pitcher Tommy Lee—a Chinese-American boy who recently moved to Metropolis. On the pitching mound, Tommy disposes of opposing hitters with his hard fastball, sweet curve, and deceptive changeup. Off the mound, he is bright, polite, and well liked by his teammates, with the notable exception of Chuck Riggs, the former pitching ace who was moved into a backup role after Tommy won the top spot. One afternoon at practice

Tommy accidently hits Chuck with a pitch. Chuck accuses Tommy of hitting him on purpose. As tempers flare, Jimmy Olsen is forced to send Chuck home to cool off.

After establishing a character that listeners could relate to, it was time to set up the villain. Enter Chuck's gruff and opinionated uncle, Matt Riggs. Riggs repeatedly insists that Tommy was trying to kill Chuck by throwing at his head. Then Matt convinces his nephew to join him at a "secret meeting" of "100 percent Americans" to be held that evening in the woods outside the city. In a secluded glade the light of a burning cross casts weird shadows over dozens of men dressed in long robes and pointed hoods. Matt—donning a white robe with a pale blue scorpion emblem on the chest—reveals himself to be the Grand Scorpion of the Clan of the Fiery Cross, a secret society dedicated to the principle of "one race, one religion and one color." As the Clansmen place their right hands over their hearts and separate the fingers of their left hands in a strange, ritualistic salute to their flaming symbol, Matt vows to rid Metropolis of all nonwhite, non-Christian "vermin" and "scum." The hooded vigilantes vow to force the Lee family out of Metropolis—or worse.

Both a sympathetic character and a detestable villain had been established. Now the time had come to drive home the moral point. After the Clan burns a cross on the Lees' front lawn, Clark Kent and Jimmy Olsen come to the aid of Tommy and his family. Clark tells Jimmy what they're up against: "The Clan of the Fiery Cross is made up of intolerant bigots, Jim. They don't judge a man in the decent American way by his own qualities. They judge him by what church he goes to or the color of his skin." Calling intolerance "a filthy weed," Clark adds that their only hope is to "hunt out the roots and pull them out of the ground."

The story also had to reveal the time-tested methods of the hooded order. As the drama unfolds, Matt Riggs calls upon the Clan's "action committee" to take care of the Lees once and for all. The next day the action committee kidnaps Tommy and takes him to a secluded cave to be tarred and feathered. As the action picks up, Tommy manages to escape his captors but breaks his arm in the scuffle. Running for his life, with the Clansmen in hot pursuit, Tommy comes to a river and, with no other choice, dives in, only to be washed downstream in a raging current. Fortunately for Tommy, Superman is searching for him in the skies above. At the last moment the caped hero swoops down to save the boy from a watery grave.

It was critical that the script go beyond Superman heroics to make the point that ordinary people can stand up to hate. This is driven home by *Daily Planet* editor Perry White, who publishes a scathing editorial condemning the Clan and offers a $1,000 reward for information leading to the apprehension of the culprits. "They can't scare me with their mumbo jumbo and burning crosses," howls the curmudgeonly editor. "I just hope this country realizes the threat posed by these lunatics in nightshirts."

Of course, standing up for what's right is not always easy. As the tale goes on, the Clan kidnaps Mr. White and Jimmy and takes them to the secluded cave, where the two abductees come face-to-face with Grand Scorpion Matt Riggs. At that point Mr. White ratchets up the moral outrage.

"Now you listen to me," Mr. White fumes. "I happen to love my country and what it stands for: equal rights and privileges for all Americans regardless of what church they choose to worship God in or what color skin God gave them," he lectures. "The United States was founded on that principle and we just fought a second world war to preserve it. You and others like you, with your diseased minds, want to tear down what we've built and fought to keep. But you can't do it. I'll fight you to my last breath and so will every other American worth his salt. We'll flush you and your hate-mongering ghouls out from behind your dirty sheets and slap you in jail where you belong."

The plot thickens. The Clan takes Mr. White and Jimmy to a secluded glade and readies their guns for the execution. Fortunately, back in Metropolis, Clark Kent and Lois Lane have been busy. They have published a special edition of the *Daily Planet* with news of the kidnapping and a plea for information about the Clan. No longer able to keep his silence, young Chuck Riggs tells Clark all he knows about the Clan of the Fiery Cross, including the role of his uncle and the whereabouts of their secret hideout. Clark secretly changes into Superman and—with a hearty "Up, Up and Away"—soars off with Chuck in his arms and searches for Mr. White, Jimmy, and the kidnappers. Just moments before the execution is to occur, Superman swoops down to save the captives. The Man of Steel rounds up the goons and takes them to the police station, only to discover that Matt Riggs escaped in the confusion.

It was also important to show that the secret organization was more than just a hate group. It was a business, as much about money as about race. This point is made as Matt Riggs goes to Graham City to meet with a Mr. Secret Wilson—Grand Imperial Mogul and Supreme National Leader of the Clan of the Fiery Cross. Matt pleads with the Imperial Mogul to call out the national action committee to finish what he started. But to Matt's astonishment, Wilson is furious. He accuses Matt of exposing the Clan to grave risk, "just when we were launching a huge, new membership drive." Wilson claims that the bad publicity "will cost us 10,000 new members who would have paid us $100 for membership fees and $25 for hoods and robes." Looking Matt in the eye, Wilson states that the Clan is really only about making money from weak and gullible men stupid enough to join it. "Is it possible that you actually believe all that stuff about getting rid of the foreigners—that one race, one religion, one color hokum?" Wilson asks Matt. "You've become drunk on the slop we put up for the suckers . . . the jerks who go for that 100 percent American rot . . . I'm running a business Riggs and so are you," Wilson rages. "We deal in one of the oldest and most profitable commodities on earth—hate."

With tension rising, Matt and Wilson struggle. Matt overpowers Wilson and, wild with fury, strangles the Imperial Mogul to death. Then Matt heads back to Metropolis to finish off his other enemies. In a moment of clarity the mad hatemonger realizes that the championship baseball game between Unity House and Metropolis High School is scheduled for the next day. That will give him an opportunity to dispose of three people who could testify against him. Chuck Riggs will be pitching for Unity House. Jimmy Olsen will be managing the team. And Mr. White will be in attendance to award a trophy to the winning team. Matt can wait to deal with Tommy Lee, who is in the hospital with the broken arm he suffered while escaping the Clan.

Finally, the time comes for the thrilling conclusion. As the game begins, Matt is on a roof overlooking the field, clutching a high-power rifle with a telescopic sight. He plans to kill Chuck, Jimmy, and Mr. White with three successive shots. Fortunately, Clark Kent is at the game and on the lookout for trouble. His x-ray eyes notice a glint of light coming from the nearby rooftop. Turning into Superman and flying faster than the speed of light just as Matt squeezes the trigger, he deflects all three bullets from their targets, flies to the roof, captures Matt, and hands him over to the police. "Three strikes and you're out," he tells Matt. The Unity House team wins the championship game, and Mr. White awards a golden baseball to Chuck—the winning pitcher. Then everyone heads to the hospital to award a duplicate trophy to Tommy.

Metropolis is safe.

The Clan of the Fiery Cross is finished.

Superman continued to stand proud into the 1970s as evidenced by this cover proclaiming it the "Best-Selling comics magazine."

CHAPTER 18

SUPERMAN, WE APPLAUD YOU

"CLAN OF THE FIERY CROSS" was an unprecedented success. The increase in ratings solidified *The Adventures of Superman* as the undisputed leader in children's radio. Praise poured in from such organizations as the United Parents' Association and the Boys' Clubs of America. When the National Conference of Christians and Jews presented Superman with an award, its vice president stated, "[We] want you, Superman, to know how grateful are all people of good will for your work in rooting out hatred." The *Radio Mirror* published a full-page tribute to the Man of Steel, "because he has done so much to show folks how important it is to respect each other's rights and to get along together." Publicity chief Hal Davis of the K&E agency laid down a gauntlet to other children's programs. "We think more shows should be doing this type of work," he dared, as Bob Maxwell placed full-page ads in trade publications proclaiming, "Here is the Nation's Answer."

Newsweek declared, "Superman is the first children's program to develop a social consciousness. Officials for both sponsor and network were relieved when the show's plea for tolerance began attracting the highest ratings in the history of the series." In the same *Newsweek* column, actor Bud Collyer officially revealed his dual identity as the voices of both Clark Kent and Superman, and he promised that the tolerance crusade would continue. Before long he would be urging groups of children to reject prejudice while on tour for the Anti-Defamation League.

Writing in the *New York World-Telegram* on September 10, 1946, Harriet Van Horne noted, "[T]he youngsters find him more exciting than ever. The show's rating goes steadily upward and the audience mail is unprecedented. Not only that Superman is receiving citations left and right from those who approve his brand new (but awfully busy) social conscience . . . It seems to me that Superman has something to say that parents, as well as kids, might well listen to."

NOT EVERYONE was thrilled, however. Anti-Semitic commentator Gerald L. K. Smith reportedly denounced Superman as "a disgrace to America," while other columnists reported that Maxwell had received death threats from the New Jersey Klan. "But Maxwell is ignoring the letter," one columnist reported, and "Superman is continuing the fight." *The Adventures of Superman* announcer Jackson Beck later recalled, "The dangers were very immediate at the time. The real life Klan had already made strong inroads in New Jersey—just across the river from our studios. They were launching a major campaign at the time to get hold of kids and promote their narrow view of what they wanted society to be like." KKK supporters in Atlanta orchestrated a phone-call campaign, generating complaints to the Mutual affiliate station in Atlanta and—according to some reports—calling for a boycott of Kellogg's cereal. Kellogg's stood by the programs and proudly announced, "Tolerance is breaking out all over Battle Creek."

In a three-part series in the *Washington Post* Sonia Stein underscored the praise and shrugged off the critics:

Of all the late afternoon little dramas for little people, Mutual's "Superman" had received most comment and most laurels—all in tribute to the year-old battle against intolerance . . . Superman's move was brave and well-intentioned . . . and it did drive the Grand Dragon of the Ku Klux Klan to try to get the sponsoring product, Pep, banned from his town. But it's doubtful that the results live up to the motivation.

Later Josette Frank, speaking at a conference of educators and broadcasters, explained that the Superman producers had tried to avoid an entanglement with the KKK and its sympathizers. Noting that Mutual affiliates in several markets did receive complaints about "The Clan of the Fiery Cross," she added that protests were small and came mostly from extremists. "When we attacked the Ku Klux Klan, for example, we got protests from a number of stations," she told the educators and broadcasters. "We didn't use a Negro. We used a Chinese boy, who simply introduced the problem of color. We hoped this would not offend the people in Atlanta but they were offended anyway, so it seems we needn't have gone out of our way. I must say the Kellogg's people backed it 100 percent and they resolutely refused to become disconcerted by the protests. Of course, by and large, there haven't been many protests and most of them have clearly come from the lunatic fringe." Miss Frank added that the response of children was inconclusive but rewarding: "There was the little Negro girl who said she found it very comforting to know that Superman was on her side."

In time the Anti-Defamation League stepped forward to make sure its man on the scene—or behind the scene—got credit. The *ADL Bulletin* of February 1947 reported, "It is now revealed that Superman's informant was Stetson Kennedy, brilliant young Southern liberal who had joined the Klan and the (neo Nazi) Columbians under the assumed name of John S. Perkins. Nowadays Kennedy is telling the whole ugly story of racism in the South and its dollar hungry peddlers, who charged him $10 for a moth-eaten, second hand Klan uniform."

Kennedy even held a press conference in full KKK garb at the ADL offices in New York. His antics apparently did not sit well with Grand Dragon Green. An April 7, 1947, report by an unnamed KKK informant claimed that Green "circulated a picture of Kennedy and said his ass is worth $1,000 per pound."

And in response to the rank and file's criticism of "failing to provide floggings, cross burnings, etc in '47," the Grand Dragon promised "a hot year in '48 if they could catch the spies."

Over the years that followed, Kennedy and other infiltrators redoubled their efforts, and the negative press continued to flow. By 1948 the Klan had become a kicking dog for a host of enemies. The governor of Florida responded to a KKK parade by calling the marchers "hooded hoodlums and sheeted jerks." And *Time* magazine reported that "a bigoted little obstetrician named Samuel Green" was becoming desperate to "prove to everybody that his movement wasn't on the skids." *Time* also noted that Green was under withering attack from such powerful opponents as the Junior Chamber of Commerce and a local group of churchwomen.

Despite a 1,500-guest birthday party for Samuel Green and despite Green's claims (reported by infiltrators) that he had 5,000 requests from all over the country to open KKK chapters, the talk of revival turned out to be just that—talk. The secret order was riddled with infiltrators, hounded by investigators, buried in bad press, and out of step with the modern mainstream of America.

IN JULY 1949, a *Nation* magazine reporter interviewed Green about the state of the Klan. Responding to the question of why the KKK always wore disguises, Green replied with a bizarre line: "So many people are prejudiced against the Klan these days."

In August 1949, Grand Dragon Samuel Green retired to his rose garden and died a quiet death. His passing threw the already compromised organization into complete disarray. There was no heir apparent with Green's background, oratory prowess, or organizational skills, and the KKK once again splintered into a disconnected set of competing factions. It would rise again, but for now, at least, it seemed that truth, justice, and the champion of the oppressed had won. The long-awaited national Klan revival would not happen, although the organization once again went underground and continued with its hateful ways in the shadows of American life.

IT'S TEMPTING to give Superman, along with the infiltrators who fed the Superman team the information, the main credit for the failure of the 1947 KKK revival. It makes a great story. But reality is, as usual, more complicated. The pressure of federal and state prosecutors, the reporting of crusading journalists, and the tenacious work of private watchdog groups such as the ADL provided the real muscle for the attack on the Klan. In addition, in the 1950s the ADL succeeded in getting many states to pass laws that prohibited the wearing of masks in public demonstrations. That way authorities could arrest Klansmen at their own gatherings. But the Superman radio campaign did mark an important milestone.

"The Clan of the Fiery Cross" showed children—and adults—all over the country the deep-seated prejudice that fueled the KKK's mission and the greed for money that motivated its leaders. And the show's use of satire and ridicule set the stage for others to use those weapons against the Klan. In years to come, national news broadcasters would invite hooded wizards and dragons onto their interview shows and let their ridiculous outfits and convoluted logic speak for themselves. Comedian Dick Gregory would develop a stand-up comedy routine ridiculing the Klan. It included this line: "A Klanner is a cat [slang for man] who gets out of bed in the middle of the night and takes his sheet with him."

The very fact that a kids' radio show could take on the dread leaders of the most persistent, most frightening homegrown hate group in the history of the United States spoke volumes about the standing of the KKK and the changes in U.S. society. In the wake of a war against one of the most evil racist organizations in history, the majority of people of all walks of life related more to a mythical superhero than to hooded vigilantes preaching superiority of one race over another.

OUT OF THE CLASH between the Man of Steel and the men of hate rose a legend, which took on a life of its own and proved as lasting as some of the folklore Stetson Kennedy recorded on his trips through the American South in the 1930s. This new folklore was apparently introduced by Kennedy, promoted by the Superman producers, and first published by Thomas Whiteside in the *New Republic* in 1946. Whiteside reported that the Superman radio show caused "a considerable amount of bad feeling among the Ku Klux Klan by mentioning various KKK code words."

Whiteside's article explained how "the code words had been passed on to Superman, via the Anti Defamation League, by Stetson Kennedy, an interloper from the newspaper *PM*. As a result Samuel Green, Grand Dragon of the KKK, had to spend part of his afternoon with his ears pressed against the radio." According to Whiteside, "As soon as Superman used a KKK code word," Green would have to notify the entire Klavern that the secret word had been compromised by a kids' radio show. Kennedy embellished the story even more in his 1954 book *I Rode with the Ku Klux Klan* (later retitled *The Klan Unmasked*), and it was soon picked up by a number of articles and books on both Superman and the Ku Klux Klan. It has been repeated ever since.

As anyone who listens to the radio shows (now available online) can tell, the myth is not true. There were no KKK code words mentioned in the series. There is evidence that Kennedy passed KKK code words on to news broadcasters, and the revelations may have irritated the Klan, but they were never aired in the Superman series. But the story has persisted, and in its own way it has served a purpose. Just as the show exposed the inner workings of the KKK to a generation of children, the myth has taught generations of people to see the KKK as foolish children playing a game of clubhouses and costumes and code words.

AFTER "THE CLAN OF THE FIERY CROSS," the Superman radio show team broadcast two more series that pitted the Man of Steel against hate groups. But Superman's attacks on hooded Klansmen and neo-Nazis thugs finally ran their course, and the writers and producers moved on to new adventures and new villains. In the ensuing years, as times changed, Superman changed with them. New writers, illustrators, and producers introduced new enemies, allies, and story lines. Over the years Superman has embodied the cultural reality of the times.

In the 1940s, when Superman teamed up with Batman, Robin, Wonder Woman, and Captain America, he taught his legions of fans how cooperation and teamwork transcended selfishness. He changed—in the more conservative 1950s—from the "champion of the oppressed" to defender of "the American way," supporting the police and the political establishment. When he retreated to his Fortress of Solitude in the Arctic, he showed us the restorative power of contemplation and the importance of knowing ourselves. His lifelong passion for and eventual marriage to Lois Lane served up a powerful lesson in love—and persistence. His refusals to join his archenemy Lex Luthor in a life of crime taught us the importance of resisting temptation and remaining true to our beliefs.

Our hero's split personality—that vast gulf between the milquetoast persona of Clark Kent and the supreme confidence of Superman—represented the full potential inherent in all human beings. It made us feel that we too could shed our day-to-day exteriors to reveal the real hero within. And Superman never let us forget that he was on our side. At the end of the 1978 film *Superman: The Movie,* he delivers Lex Luthor to prison. When the warden thanks him for making the country safe again, Superman utters these closing words:

Don't thank me, Warden.
We're all part of the same team.

And it is still so. In fact, the current Superman remains true to Jerry Siegel and Joe Shuster's original intent. In 2011, in *Action Comics* #900, Superman announces his intention to give up his U.S. citizenship, triggering waves of controversy and comment in newspapers, in magazines, and on the Internet. In that story line Superman faces the wrath of the U.S. government for supporting protesters demonstrating against the totalitarian regime in Iran. Deciding that it is more important to stand for principle than to serve any one government, the character returns to his confrontational style of the late 1930s and declares himself a citizen of the entire world.

To this day Superman has retained his place as the king of the superheroes, conquering the bad guys in comic books, TV shows, movies, and video games. He remains an all-powerful alien who stands guard against threats to human dignity and freedom and always shows us the best in ourselves.

WHAT HAPPENED TO THEM?

SUPERMAN went on to become the centerpiece of his own TV series, books, records, movies, video games, and even a rap song by Eminem. Through the years his superpowers ebbed and flowed, as did his cast of comic costars, which came to include Superboy, Supergirl, and Krypto the Superdog. Starring Christopher Reeve, the 1978 film *Superman: The Movie* launched a silver-screen Superman revival that continues to this day. A brilliant blend of creative storytelling and aggressive marketing, Superman remains the undisputed king of the superhero genre.

JERRY SIEGEL AND JOE SHUSTER sued DC Comics in 1947 for $5 million and a share of the rights to Superman. The courts ruled that Siegel and Shuster had given up any claim to ownership by assigning the rights to DC back in 1938. Joe and Jerry walked away with a $100,000 settlement (most of which went to cover legal costs) but were no longer credited as the creators of Superman. After a number of years of estrangement, Jerry divorced his first wife, Bella, in 1947. Later that year he married Joanne Carter, an actress from his hometown. Carter had once posed as a model for the Lois Lane character in the late 1930s.

After their departure from DC Comics, Jerry and Joe struggled to earn a living in comic books. They grew increasingly bitter and more destitute. In 1975 Siegel launched a publicity campaign to raise awareness of the case, and DC's parent company, Warner Communications, guaranteed both Jerry and Joe pensions of $35,000 per year for life and restored their standing as the creators. Joe Shuster died a lifelong bachelor on January 30, 1992. Jerry Siegel died on January 28, 1998. Their survivors continue to fight for a greater share of the proceeds from Superman.

ROBERT MAXWELL continued to produce the Superman radio show until it ended in 1951. He followed that successful run by creating the *Adventures of Superman* television series. The tough, realistic, dramatic Superman that Maxwell brought to TV was aimed more at adults than at the previous juvenile audience of the radio program or comic books. Maxwell left the TV series after 26 episodes and went on to launch other television programs, including the hit shows *Lassie, National Velvet, Cannonball,* and *Father of the Bride.* He died on February 3, 1971, at age 63.

STETSON KENNEDY continued his work as a writer, organizer, and agitator. He ran unsuccessfully as a write-in candidate for governor of Florida in 1951, when his friend and frequent houseguest Woody Guthrie wrote a campaign song titled "Stetson Kennedy." During the McCarthy era he came under the scrutiny of the House Un-American Activities Committee and left the United States to travel the world. He spent several years in Europe and spent time behind the Iron Curtain. While abroad he published a book entitled *I Rode with the Ku Klux Klan,* which later was rereleased as *The Klan Unmasked.* In the book he dramaticized his role as an infiltrator, crediting himself with work others—including John Brown—had done. He also added specific scenes and dialogue that he had not witnessed. When asked later why he did this, he told interviewers—including myself—that he was protecting the anonymity of these sources, whose lives would have been endangered if their roles were revealed; he also said that he wanted to give the book the air of a novel for maximum effect.

Stetson Kennedy's penchant for publicity was a hallmark of his career. During press conferences he would regale reporters with his Klan-busting exploits while dressed in a classic KKK robe and hood. In another high profile stunt, he was escorted off the grounds of the U.S. Capitol by police for seeking to visit a congressional committee—in full KKK regalia. Through it all Kennedy seemed to relish the role of rabble-rouser and continued to stir up controversy over social issues well into his 90s.

In 2005 authors Stephen Dubner and Steven D. Levitt included a favorable account of Kennedy's Klan-busting capers in their book *Freakonomics.* They based their story on Kennedy's *The Klan Unmasked* so they followed Kennedy's lead in giving him full credit for what was really a group effort. They also further spread the myth of the code words in the Superman radio show. After the book's publication a researcher and onetime Kennedy collaborator charged that Dubner and Levitt had grossly exaggerated events in their book and that Kennedy had taken credit for undercover work performed by infiltrator John Brown. Dubner and Levitt recanted much of their praise for Kennedy and wrote in the *New York Times Magazine* that they had been hoodwinked.

My account of Kennedy's role throughout this book is based on the ADL and ANL files, as well as newspaper articles from the period. It is my belief that Kennedy—while prone to exaggeration—did get very close to the KKK and worked tirelessly to expose its secrets. In addition to *The Klan Unmasked* and *Southern Exposure,* Kennedy's books include *Palmetto Country, Jim Crow Guide: The Way It Was,* and *Grits and Grunts: Folkloric Key West.* He is a founding member and past president of the Florida Folklore Society and a recipient of the 1998 Florida Folk Heritage Award and the Florida Governor's Heartland Award.

THE KU KLUX KLAN splintered into a number of competing white-supremacist organizations. While the KKK would not revive as a national organization, its various splinter groups did rise up to impose a rein of terror on civil rights advocates during the 1950s and 1960s. In the South, KKK groups used physical violence and assassination as weapons and burned crosses to intimidate opponents. Investigators traced the 1964 murders of three civil rights workers in Philadelphia, Mississippi, to the White Knights of the Ku Klux Klan, a particularly vicious offshoot. Following those infamous murders, the FBI launched a crackdown on the Klan and drove its various units further underground. KKK units—while smaller and more splintered than in the past—continue to operate to this day. In fact, the Ku Klux Klan, which just a few years ago seemed static, has stubbornly revived itself. Exploiting hot-button issues like gay marriage and urban crime, it uses the Internet to recruit followers.

SUPERMAN SOURCES

Ames, Dorothy D. "National Jewish Monthly." Vol. 61 (January 1947), 162–163.

Chabon, Michael. *The Amazing Adventures of Kavalier and Clay*. Picador, 2000.

Child Study Association of America Papers, box 220, folder 240. Josette Frank files, box 24, folder 236. Elmer L. Andersen Library, Social Welfare History Archives, Minneapolis.

Daniels, Les. *Superman: The Complete History; The Life and Times of the Man of Steel*. Chronicle Books, 1998.

———— *Wonder Woman: The Complete History; The Life and Times of the Amazon Princess*. Chronicle Books, 2004.

Fine, Herbert. "The Reign of the Super-Man." *Science Fiction*, #3 (January 1933).

Gregory, Dick. "And I Ain't Just Whistlin' Dixie." *Ebony*, August 1971, 149-151.

Hajdu, David. *The Ten-Cent Plague: The Great Comic Book Scare and How it Changed America*. Farrar, Straus and Giroux, 2008.

"The Hate Mongers Organization." Audio recording. Available online at www.archive.org/details/Superman_page09.

Hayde, Michael J. *Flights of Fantasy: The Unauthorized but True Story of Radio and TV's Adventures of Superman*. BearManor Media, 2009.

Institute for Education by Radio and Television. "Education on the Air Yearbook," conference transcript. Ohio State University, 1947.

"It's Superfight." *Newsweek* (April 29, 1946).

Jones, Gerard. *Men of Tomorrow: Geeks, Gangsters and the Birth of the Comic Book*. Basic Books, 2004.

"Kennedy Named Consultant for Famed Radio Series." *Anti-Defamation League of B'Nai B'rith Bulletin*, Vol. IX, No. 3 (March 1947).

Klein, Judith. "Addition of Social Conscience Swells Child Serial Popularity: Superman and Others Fight Undemocratic Forces; Psychologist Urges More Realism but Praises Progressiveness." *New York Herald-Tribune* (July 16, 1946).

"New Deal Achievements." American Heritage Center. Available online at www.fdheritage.org/new_deal.htm.

Nobleman, Marc Tyler. *Boys of Steel: The Creators of Superman*. Knopf, 2008.

Peck, Seymore. "Heard and Overheard, A Down-to-Earth Superman." *PM* (May 15, 1946).

Siegel, Jerry, and Joe Shuster. "How Superman Would End the War." *Look* (February 27, 1940).

————. *Action Comics*, No. 1 (June 1938).

————. *Action Comics*, No. 3 (August 1938).

————. *Action Comics*, No. 7 (December 1938).

————. *Action Comics*, No. 23 (April 1940).

"Superman's Dilemma." *Time* (April 13, 1942). Available online at www.time.com/time/magazine/article/0,9171,766523,00.html.

"Superman Homepage." Younis, Steven, ed. June 28, 2011. Available online at www.supermanhomepage.com.

Superman: The Movie. Dir. Richard Donner. Alexander Salkind, 1978. Film.

Van Horne, Harriet. "Superman's Message Is for Grownups, Too." *World Telegram* (September 10, 1946).

Wade, Wyn Craig. *The Fiery Cross: The Ku Klux Klan in America*. Oxford University Press, 1998.

Weinstein, Simcha. *Up, Up, and Oy Vey! How Jewish History, Culture, and Values Shaped the Comic Book Superhero*. Leviathan Press, 2006.

Whiteside, Thomas. "Up and Awa-a-y." *The New Republic* (March 3, 1947).

Wise, Stephen Samuel. *No Jews Need Apply*. Bloch Publishing, 1917.

Wylie, Philip. *Gladiator*. Knopf, 1930.

KU KLUX KLAN SOURCES

The American. Crowel-Collier Publishing, 1944. Vol. 137.

Buhite, Russel D., and David W. Levy, *FDR's Fireside Chats*. University of Oklahoma Press, 1992.

Bulger, Peggy. *Stetson Kennedy: Applied Folklore and Cultural Advocacy*. University of Pennsylvania, 1992.

"Calvin: Minds in the Making, Archive of Nazi Propaganda." *Das schwarze Korps* (April 25, 1940), 8. Available online at www.calvin.edu/academic/cas/gpa/superman.htm.

Chalmers, David M. *Hooded Americanism: The History of the Ku Klux Klan*. Duke University Press, 1987.

"Clan of the Fiery Cross." Audio recording. Available online at www.archive.org/details/Superman_page09.

Davis, Susan Lawrence. *Authentic History: Ku Klux Klan 1865–1877*. American Library Service, 1924.

Deutsch, Albert. "Southern Liberals Gather Strength in Fight Against Hate Groups." *PM* (October 16, 1946).

"The Golden Era of Indiana 1900–1930." Center for History. Available online at www.centerforhistory.org.

Golden, Reuel. *New York: Portrait of a City*. Taschen, 2010.

Kennedy, Stetson. *American Memory Project: Florida Folklife from the WPA Collections, 1937 to 1942*. Library of Congress. Available online at http://memory.loc.gov/ammem/collections/florida/ffpres01.html.

———. Interview with John Egerton. May 11, 1990. Documenting the American South. Southern Oral History Program Collection (#4007). Interview No. A-0354. Available online at http://docsouth.unc.edu/sohp/A-0354/menu.html.

———. *The Klan Unmasked*. Florida Atlantic University Press, 1954.

———. *Southern Exposure*. Florida Atlantic University Press, 1991.

"Klan Sleuth Gives Superman Secrets of the Hooded Order." *Anti-Defamation League of B'Nai B'rith Bulletin*, Vol. IX, No. 2 (February 1947).

"National Affairs: The Better Element." *Time* (June 14, 1948). Available online at www.time.com/time/magazine/article/0,9171,800286,00.htm.

"The New Jersey Hall of Shame." Available online at www.njhallofshame.com/FrameSet.html.

Nietzsche, Friedrich. "The Birth of Tragedy." In *Basic Writings of Nietzsche*. Kaufmann, Walter, trans. Modern Library Edition, 2000.

Non-Sectarian Anti-Nazi League Investigative Files, Columbia University Library, Rare Book and Manuscripts, New York, NY. Box 1519.

Rice, Arnold S. *The Ku Klux Klan in American Politics*. Public Affairs Press, 1962.

Risel, Victor. "KKK Activity Stirred by Anti-Religious Violence." *Labor News and Comment* (January 14, 1944).

Smith, Jean Edward. *FDR*. Random House, 2009.

"Stetson Kennedy, Author of Book Exposing Klan Visits St. Petersburg." *St. Petersburg Times* (January 22, 1948).

Stetson Kennedy Papers. Schomburg Center for Research in Black Culture, New York Public Library, New York, NY.

———. *New York Times* website. Available online at http://graphics8.nytimes.com/images/blogs/freakonomics/pdf/stetson1.pdf.

Wall, Wendy L. *Inventing the American Way: The Politics of Consensus from the New Deal to the Civil Rights Movement*. Oxford Press, 2009.

★ SOURCES ★

Chapter 1
p. 13, "No Jews need apply": Wise, 1; p. 14, "100 percent Americanism": Chalmers, 57.

Chapter 2
p. 20, "With a contemptuous sneer": Fine, 1; p. 26, "The most astounding": Daniels, 17.

Chapter 3
p. 30, "the only thing": Smith, 278; p. 30, "a new deal": Smith, 333; p. 31, "hazards and vicissitudes of life": Wall, 37; p. 31, "to the average citizen": "New Deal Achievements"; p. 31, "mere crumbs": Ibid.; p. 31, "share the wealth": "Ibid.; p. 31, "A few timid people": Buhite, 333.

Chapter 5
p. 40, "A rather immature piece of work": Daniels, *Superman*, 26; p. 41, "Superman!" "Champion": Siegel and Shuster, *Action Comics* No. 1, 1; p. 41, "As a distant planet": Ibid.; p. 42, "a passing motorist": Ibid.; p. 42, "including lifting a chair": Ibid.; p. 42, "Nothing less than": Ibid.; p. 42, "turn his titanic strength": Ibid.; "The most astounding": Daniels, 17; p. 42, "Evelyn Curry": Siegel and Shuster, *Action Comics* No. 1, 3; p. 43, "Gentlemen, I still": Ibid., 4; p. 43, "with a sharp snap": Ibid., 6; p. 43, "You're going to": Ibid., 6; p. 43, "see how": Siegel and Shuster, *Action Comics* No. 3, 7; p. 43, "people actually": Ibid., 8; p. 43, "Knee deep": Ibid., 11; p. 44, "safest mine": Ibid., 11; p. 44, "And so begins": Siegel and Shuster, *Action Comics* No. 1, 13; p. 45, "Friend of the helpless": Siegel and Shuster, *Action Comics* No. 7, 1.

Chapter 6
p. 49, "One of the mounted Knights": Kennedy, *Klan Unmasked*, 17; p. 50, "It happened early": Kennedy, Stetson. Interview with John Egerton., 2; p. 51, "I've always felt like an alien": Ibid., 3; p. 51, "I do believe": Ibid., 6; p. 51, "As a matter of fact": Ibid; p. 51, "a dollar down and a dollar a week": Ibid., 3; p. 52, "Don't ask me": Ibid.; p. 52, "We traveled the backroads": Kennedy, "American Memory Project"; p. 53, "a kid on a treasure": Ibid.; p. 53," Dear Lord,

this is Eartha White": Ibid.; p. 53, "Why don't you": Ibid.; "the onliest way": Ibid.; p. 54, "melt the cultural glue": Bulger, "Stetson Kennedy," 201; p. 54, "The main idea": Ibid., 189.

Chapter 7
p. 57, "*kuklos*": Chalmers, 9; p. 60, "perverted": Ibid., 19.

Chapter 8
p. 63, "ineffectiveness and moral failings": Ibid., 29; p. 64, "fraternalist": Ibid., 29; p. 65, "The Greatest Fraternal Organization": Ibid., 30.

Chapter 9
p. 71, "Now let the": Chalmers, 33; p. 72, "the poor, the romantic": Rice, 15; p. 72, "a 100-percent knife": Rice, 19; p. 73, "I am the law": "The Golden Era of Indiana."

Chapter 10
p. 81, "smooch": Jones, 88; p. 84, "Hiya Superman": Ibid., 159.

Chapter 11
p. 88, Sterling North quotes: Hajdu, 41; p. 90, "The principles of the Bund": Chalmers, 323; p. 90, "Burn Hitler on your cross": *New Jersey Hall of Shame* website.

Chapter 12
p. 93, "Faster than an airplane": *The Superman Homepage*, 1932 to 1950, the radio program; p. 94, "blood and thunder": Hayde, 82; p. 95, "Pep, the sunshine cereal": *The Superman Homepage*; p. 95, "Up, up and away!": Ibid.; p. 96, "the next thrilling episode": Ibid.; p. 96, "This looks like a job for": Jones, 159; p. 97, "the Superman"; "flies in the marketplace": Nietzsche, 52.

Chapter 13
p. 99, "How Superman Would End the War": Siegel and Shuster, "How Superman Would End the War," online at http://www.superman.nu; p. 100, "I'd like to land": Ibid.; p. 100, "Superman ist ein Jude!":

★ SOURCES ★

"Calvin, Minds in the Making"; p. 100, "Jerry Siegel, an intellectually and physically": Ibid.; p. 102, "Superman's Dilemma": *Time,* http://www.time.com/time/magazine/article/0,9171,766523,00.html; p. 103, "What if they were"; "Would you let"; "Super-Soldiers"; *The Superman Homepage,* http://www.supermanhomep..com/comics/comics.php?topic=articles/sues-war; p. 104, "You're my Supermen": Ibid.; p. 105, "Superman got a high priority rating": "Superman's Dilemma," *Time.*

Chapter 14
p. 107, "I resolved to fight": Bulger, "Stetson Kennedy", 187; p. 108, "I had to remember": Ibid., 189; p. 109, "There are not many": *The American,* 90.

Chapter 15
p. 116, "We're not in the business . . ." *PM,* May 15, 1946, 5; p. 117, "You'll lose your audience": Ames, "National Jewish Monthly."; p. 118, "The difficulty was": *PM,* 5; p. 119, "shaping a new form of education"; "heroes for heroism's sake"; "kids are invested": Child Study Association of America papers; p. 119, "I am seething"; "drop their baseball bats"; "Only the children": Ibid.; p. 120, "This feature does": Daniels, *Wonder Woman,* 61–62; p. 120, "Get strong": Child Study Association of America Papers; p. 120, "stories dramatizing": Ibid.; p. 120, "inappropriate to the building up of serene attitudes": Ibid.; p. 120, "What makes you think": Ibid.; p. 120, "Yes, it's Superman": Hayde, 70; p. 121, "The Hate Mongers Organization": Hayde, 71; p. 121, Summary of "The Hate Mongers Organization," Audio of original broadcast; p. 123, "Remember this as long as you live": Hayde, 70; p. 123, "use of children's own favorite medium": Ibid., 74; p. 123, "this noble effort": Ibid.; p. 123, "follow the lead": Ibid.

Chapter 16
p. 125, "We are revived": Wade, 277; p. 126, "100 percent Americans": Chalmers, 57; p. 127, "sloshing over": Chalmers, 333; p. 127, "To his majesty": Bulger, "Stetson Kennedy," 198; p. 129, "This worker is joining": Stetson Kennedy Papers, *New York Times;* p. 129, "write a letter": Non-Sectarian

Anti Nazi League collection; p.130, "our informant is now": Ibid.; p. 131, "fabulous jet propelled character": Kennedy, *The Klan Unmasked,* 92; p. 131, "Armed with complete information": Ibid.

Chapter 17
p. 134-39, Summary of "The Clan of the Fiery Cross": Audio of original broadcast.

Chapter 18
p. 141, "[We] want you, Superman": Hayde, 73; p. 141, "because he has done so much": Hayde, 72; p. 141, "Here is the Nation's Answer": Hayde, 76; p. 141, "Superman is the first": "It's Superfight," 61; p. 142, "The youngsters find him": Harriet Van Horne, *New York World-Telegram;* p. 142, "a disgrace to America": Whiteside, 15; p. 142, "But Maxwell"; "The dangers were": Hayde, 78; p. 143, "Of all the": Stein, It's Parents, Not Kids that Worry Radio, the *Washington Post,* April 20, 1947, S5; p. 143, "Tolerance is breaking": Hayde, 78; p. 143-44, "When we attacked"; "We didn't use a negro"; "There was the little": Institute for Education, Education on the Air, 157–158; p. 144, "It is now revealed that": "Kennedy Named," *ADL Bulletin,* February 1947, 7; p. 144, "circulated a picture": Stetson Kennedy Papers, Schomberg Center, KKK Infiltrator Reports; p. 144, "failing to provide floggings"; "a hot year in '48": Ibid.; p. 144, "hooded hoodlums and sheeted jerks": Chalmers, 333; p. 144, "a bigoted little": "National Affairs," *Time;* p. 145, "So many people are": Chalmers, 333; p. 146, "A Klanner is a cat": Gregory, 149; p. 147, "a considerable amount": Whiteside, 15-17; p. 147, "the code words": Ibid.; p. 147, "As soon as Superman": Ibid.; p. 148, "Champion of the Oppressed": Siegel and Shuster, *Action Comics* No. 1, 1; p. 148, "the American way": Daniels, 18; p. 149, "Don't thank me": *Superman: The Movie.*